TESTIMONIALS

A big congratulations to Penny. This book will be a very valuable resource to anyone seeking to understand and learn how to grow their private practice. I had the privilege to learn from Penny as my supervisor and also in attending the workshop she ran on the fundamentals of Private Practice, which has been invaluable. Rebranding my Private Practice was a big step and, at times, overwhelming. I reached out to Penny to help me set up my business and navigate the new season and it was very beneficial. Penny has extensive knowledge and experience in this space, so learning from her firsthand and hearing about her own personal journey has been encouraging. The workshop and the workbook she created provided me with a framework, manageable steps and simple goals that made building my Private Practice more achievable and less intimidating.

Thank you, Penny, for all your input and encouragement along the way. I appreciate your support, non-judgmental stance, kindness and valuable pointers. I am looking forward to getting my copy of the book and will be recommending it to fellow counsellors within the industry. Thank you for sharing your wisdom with all of us.

Rebecca Royle
Counsellor
Arukah Counselling and Family Therapy
www.arukahcounselling.com.au

The Counsellors Chair

After trying a couple of different supervisors, I found Penny Adams and I am so grateful that I did. For the past couple of years, Penny has been an ongoing source of knowledge and support that has really enhanced my counselling skills and business development. She has a rich and deep knowledge base that I haven't found elsewhere, and I really appreciate this. If you want a thoughtful, kind, honest, and super-smart supervisor, Penny is definitely the person for you. Supervision is so vital to our work, and Penny is truly excellent at her craft.

Thalia O'Sullivan
Counsellor

I believe this book will be an invaluable resource for anyone going into private practice. Penny has drawn on her wealth of experience and offers clear and practical guidance while demonstrating a wonderful understanding of the challenges and successes in private practice. This book is an excellent guide from someone who is a trusted mentor and is consistently sought after for her private practice workshops. Penny has a passion for supporting fellow counsellors in this area. This book reflects her practical insights and supportive approach.

Laura Boucher
Counsellor and Supervisor
Change For You Counselling
www.counselling4change.au

THE COUNSELLORS
Chair

THE PROVEN FRAMEWORK FOR PRIVATE PRACTICE SUCCESS

Penny Adams

First published by Ultimate World Publishing 2025
Copyright © 2025 Penny Adams

ISBN

Paperback: 978-1-923425-21-7
Ebook: 978-1-923425-22-4

Penny Adams has asserted her rights under the Copyright, Designs and Patents Act 1988 to be identified as the author of this work. The information in this book is based on the author's experiences and opinions. The publisher specifically disclaims responsibility for any adverse consequences which may result from use of the information contained herein. Permission to use information has been sought by the author. Any breaches will be rectified in further editions of the book.

All rights reserved. No part of this publication may be reproduced, stored in or introduced into a retrieval system, or transmitted in any form, or by any means (electronic, mechanical, photocopying, recording or otherwise) without the prior written permission of the author. Any person who does any unauthorised act in relation to this publication may be liable to criminal prosecution and civil claims for damages. Enquiries should be made through the publisher.

Cover design: Ultimate World Publishing
Layout and typesetting: Ultimate World Publishing
Editor: Rebecca Low

Ultimate World Publishing
Diamond Creek,
Victoria Australia 3089
www.writeabook.com.au

Testimonials

Penny Adams, what a legend! Penny was one of my lecturers. Once graduated, she also assisted me in designing my website, and then created it for me. Penny's business course was full of encouragement, great content, wisdom and knowledge of the counselling/business industry. Penny's course was just what I needed to start me on the road to launching my own private practice with confidence because of her proven approach to all aspects of the industry. This book will be a golden nugget for all who want to make a difference in their counselling profession.

Betty Ross
Counsellor
BR Counselling Care
www.brcounsellingcare.com.au

I have had the pleasure of knowing and benefiting from Penny's vast wealth of experience for which I am so grateful. Penny has a strong dedication to her craft and to the industry at large which has set her apart from other counsellors and supervisors. On more than one occasion, I have benefited from Penny's guidance and been able to elevate my own professional business and personal development to greater heights than I had expected. Penny genuinely cares about you and your success which is so refreshing and comforting, especially when just starting out in the industry. As a supervisor, Penny is approachable, respectful and caring but not afraid to correct you if she notices you heading in the wrong direction. Thanks, Penny, for all you are and everything you have done and continue to do for me, you are very much appreciated and valued.

Peter Grimes
Counsellor, Supervisor, Trainer
Peter Grimes Online Counselling
www.petergrimesonlinecounselling.com.au

The Counsellors Chair

Having worked closely with Penny in various counsellor training roles, I can attest to her remarkable in-depth knowledge of the profession and her natural ability to communicate with insight, encouragement, enthusiasm, warmth and humour.

I am continually in awe of Penny's diligence to remain current with evolving industry standards, training pathways and association requirements. Her commitment to ongoing learning ensures she is a trusted voice of wisdom in the counselling field.

For over ten years, I have witnessed Penny's unwavering dedication to the advancement of the counselling profession, particularly her passion for nurturing and supporting new counsellors. She is a true champion for both emerging and experienced professionals, inspiring them to grow, flourish and succeed.

Writing this book seems a natural next step in her journey and it is with great excitement I congratulate Penny on this achievement.

Deb McKee
Counsellor and Supervisor
Purple Lemon Counselling
www.purplelemoncounselling.com.au

Testimonials

Penny has been an integral part of my counselling journey. She has been a trustworthy teacher and supervisor, generously helping me through every aspect of setting up my private practice. Her support and impartation have been practical and ethical. As a result, I have a thriving practice. Thank you, Penny!

Sharne Kilsby
Counsellor and Supervisor
Shiloh Within Counselling
www.shilohwithincounselling.com.au

Penny's private practice workshop was hands down the best investment I made when beginning my private practice. It was so practical and thorough. I recommend it to everyone starting out now. This book will be an amazing resource! Universities should make the book essential reading, as the business side of running a counselling practice is often omitted from our training. Thank you, Penny, for all that you contribute to the counselling community. You're a gem!

Shelley Bell
Counsellor
Branch of Hope Counselling
www.branchofhope.com.au

DEDICATION

Firstly, to God, the author and creator of all. To my family, my husband, Ben, and my two beautiful daughters, Brooke and Emma, your love and support have been my anchor through every season of this journey. To my parents, not a day goes by where I don't wish for just one more conversation with you. Your absence has shaped me in ways I never expected, and without that loss, I may not be writing this book.

CONTENTS

Testimonials	iii
Dedication	ix
Forewords	1
Disclaimer	9
Introduction	11
Chapter 1: The Counsellor's Chair: The Framework That Holds Everything Together	25
Chapter 2: Meet Counsellor Casey	31
Chapter 3: Mindset & Momentum: The Investment That Powers Your Journey	37
Chapter 4: Solid Legs: The Four Foundations of Success	63
Chapter 5: The Seat of Operations	97
Chapter 6: Marketing Backrest – Support for Business Growth	111
Chapter 7: Strong Armrests: Confident Clinical Processes	147
Chapter 8: Protective Wings – Self-Care That Prevents and Restores	175
Afterword	185
Next Steps	187
Speaker Bio	192
About the Author	193
Acknowledgements	197
More Testimonials	199

FOREWORDS

I'm Tracey Milson, a clinically registered counsellor, family therapist, supervisor, trainer, educator, and one of Penny's counselling supervisors. I've been in private clinical practice for 25 years and have conducted over 22,000 hours of counselling, supervision, and supervision of supervision.

I first met Penny whilst working in the vocational sector as a trainer and assessor where Penny was on staff. At the time, Penny was also working as a well-respected and experienced school counsellor. Since 2018, I've had the privilege of being one of Penny's primary clinical supervisors for her private client work and the supervised supervision of her counsellors.

Over this period, I've observed and recorded Penny's incredible expertise in conducting her extensive counselling businesses. This includes her client work, online practice, supervision, private practice mentoring, counselling and supervision training delivery, as well as her successful partnership with the Counsellors Community Australia (CCA) online group.

Her ethical support and guidance of others in the counselling profession are above reproach. She has modelled her success well, coupled with continuing education including accomplishing both vocational and tertiary qualifications. She 'walks the talk' as the saying goes. Some of the keys to Penny's success, from my supervision perspective, have been her positive determination to get it right, do the right thing, and influence others in the profession. Her passion for equipping counsellors aligns strongly with her desire to see clients manage their life struggles more successfully. She honestly and truly cares, which is evidenced by her committed desire to share her knowledge. This book is a testimony to her dedication to help others.

Penny has graciously and transparently shared her overall journey toward success, with advice to avoid pitfalls and the generous offer of excellent tools for business and private practice growth from a practical and workable framework. As a compilation of Penny's vast years of professional experience, this book is an essential and vital practical guide that will assist counsellors to strive for success and thrive at any stage of their career development. *The Counsellors Chair* is a must-read as one of Australia's first down-to-earth practical guides with well-honed tips and pointers for you to also conduct a successful, profitable, and sustainable, private practice business in counselling, mentoring, and the supervising of others.

Congratulations Penny on your amazing contribution to the counselling and helping profession, to assist other counsellors and therapists to have the confidence backed with tried-and-true practical methods for success from someone who truly knows how it's done with ethical integrity. This book is a fantastic people helpers aid, and an essential read!

Tracey Milson
Counsellor, Supervisor, Educator and Trainer
www.traceymilson.com.au

Forewords

Private practice is an exciting time for counsellors to embark on, yet often many are overwhelmed before they even commence. Counsellors enter the field with a deep passion for helping others yet find themselves unprepared for the intricacies of running a successful practice. Penny understands this challenge firsthand as a professional who has experienced employment in the industry and then embarked on her own journey in private practice. In her book, *The Counsellor's Chair*, Penny draws on her experience and knowledge to deliver an essential guide that outlines the path to building a sustainable, ethical, and profitable counselling practice.

I'm Rosie Barbara, a clinical counsellor, supervisor, trainer, and mentor with over two decades of experience in the counselling industry. I first met Penny through her group supervision for supervisors. From our very first conversation, I knew she was someone who was deeply committed to the growth and success of counsellors in Australia. After a couple of Zoom chats, we joined forces and together, we built the *Counsellors Community Australia* Facebook group, which flourished into a thriving space for connection and support. This collaboration naturally led to our next venture together, *Circle*, an online community designed to provide Australian counsellors with networking, learning, and essential resources to navigate their careers with confidence.

Through our years of working closely together, I have seen Penny's tireless dedication to the counselling profession. She is not only a skilled practitioner but also a strategic thinker with an ability to break down complex concepts into actionable steps. Her expertise in private practice development is substantial—she has walked the walk, investing in her own self-development, learning and business growth so she can share her knowledge with others. Penny is a leader, a mentor, and a generous advocate for counsellors.

The Counsellor's Chair truly stands out due to its unique framework. Penny presents private practice as a well-structured chair—each part representing a crucial pillar for success: stability, operations, clinical confidence, and longevity. This metaphor not only makes the concepts easy to understand but also provides a practical roadmap for those stepping into or refining their practice. The book tackles the real challenges counsellors face, from navigating business structures to defining a niche and marketing. It goes beyond generic advice, offering tailored insights specific to the counselling profession.

One of the standout aspects of Penny's approach is her no-nonsense, down-to-earth delivery. She strips away the fluff and speaks directly to what it takes to create a thriving practice. Whether you are just starting out or seeking to refine your existing practice, this book is an invaluable resource that you will refer to for years to come.

Penny Adams is a true leader in the Australian counselling industry. She has committed herself to not only building her own success but ensuring others have the information they need to achieve theirs. *The Counsellor's Chair* is a testament to her dedication, and I wholeheartedly recommend it to every counsellor ready to embark on their own journey in private practice.

Rosie Barbara
Counsellor, Supervisor, Community Co-Founder
www.rosiebarbara.com.au

Forewords

My name is Sarah, and my journey has taken me from corporate marketing into the world of coaching, mentoring, and business development to support small businesses. Over the years, I have had the privilege of working with professionals across industries, helping them build businesses that align with their values while achieving sustainable success. My experience in digital marketing, business strategy, and coaching has given me a unique perspective on the challenges that service-based professionals, particularly counsellors, face when setting up and growing their private practice.

I have worked closely with Penny for over three years as a coach and mentor, and over the past 12 months, I have been actively supporting her community. Whether through professional networks or mutual collaborations, it was clear from the outset that Penny had an extraordinary depth of knowledge and a real heart for helping counsellors succeed—not just in their clinical work but in running a business that allows them to thrive.

I have had the opportunity to engage with Penny in multiple capacities, through mentoring, professional discussions, and business strategy conversations. Penny's expertise in private practice is nothing short of impressive. She has an innate ability to break down complex business concepts into actionable strategies that work for counsellors who may not have a business background.

What stands out most about Penny is her deep understanding of the specific challenges that counsellors face—not just in terms of attracting clients but also in balancing ethical considerations, setting sustainable fees, and avoiding burnout. Her approach is both practical and compassionate, ensuring that counsellors don't just build businesses but create practices that serve both their clients and their own well-being.

Through her frameworks, particularly *The Counsellor's Chair*, she has provided countless professionals with the tools they need to not only navigate private practice but also to do so with confidence and clarity. Her work has influenced and supported many, offering a roadmap that balances professional integrity with business sustainability.

This book is an essential resource for any counsellor looking to build or grow their private practice. One of the greatest challenges new and growing counsellors face is transitioning from being a skilled clinician to becoming a confident business owner. Many struggle with pricing, marketing, and setting boundaries—areas that are critical for long-term success but are often overlooked in traditional counselling training.

Penny's approach ensures that counsellors are equipped not only with the right knowledge but also with the mindset shifts necessary to embrace their role as business owners. Her practical frameworks help demystify the business side of private practice, making it accessible and achievable for those who may feel overwhelmed by the thought of marketing, pricing, or business planning.

One key insight from this book that truly stands out is Penny's emphasis on aligning business practices with personal and professional values. Too often, counsellors feel they have to choose between being ethical and being profitable, but Penny shows that these two things can and should go hand in hand.

I would highly recommend this book to any counsellor, whether they are just starting out or looking to refine and grow their existing practice. It is a must-read for those who want a clear, structured, and supportive guide to building a practice that is both professionally fulfilling and financially sustainable.

Forewords

Penny's contribution to the counselling profession cannot be overstated. She has taken what is often an overwhelming and isolating experience—running a private practice—and turned it into a structured, supportive, and empowering journey. Her wisdom, experience, and generosity in sharing her knowledge will undoubtedly have a lasting impact on the profession for years to come.

Sarah Thomson
Speaker | Trainer | Multi-Award Winning Digital Marketing Coach | Business Mentor
www.onlinesocialbutterfly.com.au

DISCLAIMER

The information provided in this book is for informational and educational purposes only. While every effort has been made to ensure the accuracy and relevance of the content, it is not a substitute for professional, legal, financial, or business advice.

Building and running a private counselling practice involves multiple variables, many of which are unique to your circumstances. Success, including income, profit, or client acquisition cannot be promised or guaranteed. The strategies and insights shared here are designed to provide guidance and practical tools, but their effectiveness depends entirely on your own implementation, effort, and commitment.

Before making any business, legal, financial, or ethical decisions, it is strongly recommended that you consult with the appropriate professionals, such as:

- Your professional association for ethical, scope of practice, and industry regulations.

- Your business or professional indemnity insurer to confirm coverage for your services and business structure.

- A qualified accountant or financial advisor for tax, financial planning, and business structuring advice.

- A lawyer for contracts, legal obligations, and risk management.

By reading and applying the content of this book, you acknowledge that you are responsible for your own practice, decisions, and outcomes. The author and the publisher accept no liability for any direct or indirect consequences resulting from the use of this material.

INTRODUCTION

This book is unapologetically for Australian counsellors!

There's plenty of business advice out there for mental health professionals, but most of it isn't written for us. Instead, it's designed for psychologists, social workers, or therapists in other countries, leaving Australian counsellors trying to piece together fragments of information that don't quite fit our reality.

If you're a counsellor in Australia, whether you're just starting out, feeling stuck, or looking to refine your practice, this book is for you.

Private practice isn't just about being a great counsellor, it's about understanding how to build a practice that actually works. One that serves your clients, sustains you financially, and allows you to create a business that's both ethical and fulfilling. But without that knowledge, many counsellors find themselves feeling overwhelmed, uncertain, or burnt out.

That's why this book exists.

Now, if you're reading this from overseas or come from a different mental health background, you may still find useful insights here. The principles of business, sustainability, and ethical practice apply across professions. But let's be clear, this book wasn't written for you.

It was written for Australian counsellors because we deserve a roadmap that reflects our industry, and our unique challenges and opportunities.

Why I Wrote This Book

This book didn't come from a single moment of inspiration, it came from years of conversations with counsellors at all stages of their private practice journey.

When I first ran the Private Practice Fundamentals workshop, I expected a good response. But what I didn't expect was just how deeply counsellors were searching for clear, practical guidance, something that didn't promise the world but was actually useful and applicable.

I kept hearing the same frustrations:

- 'I still don't know how to actually make private practice work.'
- 'I know I'm a good counsellor, but I don't know how to attract the right clients.'
- 'I feel like I'm missing something, but I don't know what it is.'

Introduction

I realised that so many incredible, highly skilled counsellors were held back, not by a lack of talent or passion, but by a lack of accessible, straightforward business knowledge that isn't hidden behind expensive and flashy sales techniques.

I'm committed to helping Australian counsellors succeed in private practice, but I also know there's only so much I can do through supervision, training, and workshops. There's only one of me, and there are thousands of you.

By writing this book, I can give you a solid, structured foundation, something you can return to whenever you need clarity, direction or a pep-talk. Now, will this book be the only resource you ever need to establish your private practice? Definitely not. You will still need mentors, supervision, or additional training along the way. What this book will do is give you the understanding and self-assurance to make well-thought-out decisions for your practice, rather than feeling like you're navigating in the dark.

I've made the mistakes. I've had the hard moments. I know what it's like to wonder if you're doing it all wrong. But, I also know what it's like to push through, learn what works, and build something sustainable. My goal isn't just to share what I've learned, it's to help you create a private practice that works for you.

What to Expect from This Book

This isn't a business or academic textbook, and it's certainly not filled with empty motivation about simply 'believing in yourself'.

This book is practical and requires action—from you!

It's designed to give you clear, actionable steps to build and grow your private practice in a way that aligns with your values, strengths, and goals.

Through these pages, you'll gain a real understanding of the business side of private practice, without feeling like you're losing yourself in the process. You'll learn how to price your services with confidence, market authentically, and attract the right clients, all in a way that feels authentic and ethical.

More importantly, this book will help you navigate the challenges that hold many counsellors back, the mindset blocks, the self-doubt, and the fear of stepping outside your comfort zone. Success in private practice isn't just about having the right strategies, it's about having the right mindset to apply them.

What you won't find here are sunshine and lollipop promises, or one-size-fits-all solutions as every counsellor is different and every practice is unique.

There's no single 'correct' way to run a private practice. What works for one counsellor may not work for another. My job isn't to give you a rigid formula, it's to help you discover what works best for you.

You also won't find sugar-coated hype or shortcuts. Starting and growing a private practice takes time and energy, and it requires being open to learning and adjusting as you go. But with the right approach, it's absolutely possible to build a financially viable, professionally rewarding, and personally fulfilling practice.

This isn't a book to read and set aside. It's a book to use, implement, and return to whenever you need guidance, reassurance, or direction.

Introduction

This is your journey, and my hope is that this book becomes a trusted companion as you navigate the path ahead.

How This Book is Structured

This book is designed around the Counsellor's Chair Analogy, a practical framework I created that breaks private practice down into the essential parts that hold it together. Just like a chair needs sturdy legs, a comfortable seat, and a supportive backrest, a private practice needs a strong foundation, solid operations, effective marketing, ethical clinical practice, and self-care that supports and protects. Each chapter focuses on one of these elements, giving you clear, actionable steps to strengthen that part of your practice.

You'll also meet Counsellor Casey, a fictional but very real-to-life counsellor who has been inspired by the many counsellors I've worked with, whose journey weaves through this book. Casey's experiences will help bring these concepts to life, showing you what works, what doesn't, and how to navigate the common challenges counsellors face when starting and growing a private practice.

At the end of each chapter, you'll find practical action steps designed to help you take what you've learned and apply it to your own practice.

This book is here to support you, no matter where you are in your private practice journey. If you're just starting out, I encourage you to start at the beginning. Like any solid structure, a private practice needs a strong foundation. Skipping ahead might leave gaps that could make things more challenging later on. By working through the book in order, you'll build a solid base of knowledge and confidence that'll serve you well as your practice grows.

If you're already somewhere along the journey, you can choose your own adventure! Maybe you're feeling stuck when it comes to marketing, or maybe it's the business side of things that's making you hesitate. Whatever it is, jump straight to the chapters that address your biggest challenges right now.

Creating a private practice isn't a cookie-cutter journey. What works for one counsellor won't necessarily work for another, and your practice should reflect your strengths, values, and goals.

This book is here to help you navigate that journey, whether you're laying the groundwork, refining what you've built, or strengthening areas that need more attention.

No matter where you are, the key is to keep learning, keep adapting, and keep going.

Life Before Counselling

Before counselling became my career and passion, I had no idea that I'd one day be running a business, leading a community, or even working in mental health. I started my career in customer service and retail management, where I quickly learned how to handle tricky situations, connect with people, and juggle the daily chaos. If nothing else, working in retail teaches patience!

In my early 30s, I stepped away from paid work to raise my two daughters. My husband, a FIFO worker, was away six months of the year, so I often managed home life solo. The FIFO lifestyle comes with a unique set of challenges and rewards, but it also gave me time to reflect on what I wanted next.

Introduction

But my journey into counselling didn't just happen, it was shaped by deep personal loss. In the early 1990s, I lost both my parents within three months of each other, at the age of 23. My world as I knew it shattered, and I experienced heart-breaking grief and loss. It wasn't a time of great mental health support; I had no guidance from anyone on how to navigate this tragedy and I stumbled (pretty severely at times) through life for the next few years.

After I had children, I finally sought counselling for myself and discovered just how powerful and healing the process could be. It was the first time someone had really understood the pain I had experienced and it made me realise something heartbreaking, I wished I had that kind of support back when my parents died.

Those years of counselling didn't just help me heal, they planted a seed in me—to be a person who could walk alongside others in their darkest times, just as my counsellor had done for me. The experience of losing my parents changed everything and created a desire in me to help others through their pain and tragedy and to create a space where people can feel heard and understood. That birthed my decision to study counselling.

Early Counselling Career

When I started out as a counsellor, I wasn't sure where I wanted it to take me. I always said, 'I will never work with children!'

Guess what? God has a sense of humour, and I started my career working in schools, supporting students through the emotional, social, and academic challenges of school life. School counselling was rewarding but demanding, and over the years, I worked in both the private and public school systems, ranging from nearly full-time to contract work.

I loved connecting with young people and seeing their growth, but I also saw firsthand how stretched the school system was when it came to providing meaningful mental health support. There were limitations on how much time I could give to each student, and I often felt like there was so much more I could do if only I had more flexibility and autonomy.

At the same time, I was also involved in counsellor education, working for a registered training organisation (RTO) where I trained aspiring counsellors. For seven years, I worked with students at diploma, advanced diploma and graduate diploma levels, from those just starting out to those refining their skills before heading into the workforce. I absolutely loved teaching and mentoring new counsellors, helping them develop both the confidence and competence to step into the profession.

My time in education and supervision gave me a unique insight into what makes a strong, ethical, and effective counsellor. I saw the common struggles students faced, like imposter syndrome, self-doubt, and lack of business knowledge, and I knew that many of these challenges didn't disappear once they graduated but instead intensified.

Looking back, those early experiences (as hard as they were), both personal and professional, laid the foundation for who I am today. They shaped my empathy, resilience, and commitment to creating safe spaces for others to explore their pain and find hope. They also prepared me, unknowingly, for the many roles I'd take on as a counsellor, supervisor, and business owner.

Introduction

Starting Out in Private Practice

When I first stepped into private practice, I had no idea what I was doing. Seriously, less than no idea. I had been employed my whole life, and the thought of running a business felt as foreign as joining a circus (and if you know me, you know that joining a circus has never been one of my life aspirations).

In 2018, burnout hit me hard. I had been working as a school counsellor for quite some time, but the emotional load had taken its toll. I decided to take a year off to rest and figure out what was next. That's when I thought, why not give private practice a go?

My brilliant plan? Partnering with a church to provide counselling. I quickly learned two things:

1. Not many people in that rural town wanted to go to a church for counselling.
2. I still wasn't fully in charge of my business.

By 2019, I left the church partnership and officially launched Seasons of Life Counselling.

Overcoming Challenges

Let's not pretend it's been smooth sailing. In 2019, I managed to dislocate my knee and ankle (on opposite legs, because why not?) while on holiday. It impacted me significantly for nearly six months, affecting both my school job and private practice. I'm stubborn, so I kept going, but the effects have stayed with me, and I now juggle ongoing pain and a pinched nerve in my back.

Balancing family life with business was another challenge. My two daughters were in high school when I started, and my husband worked FIFO, so free time was something I'd heard of but never experienced. Even now, with my girls off forging their own paths in life, finding time to be a business owner versus just a counsellor is an ongoing challenge.

Oh, and did I mention I'm an introvert? Let's just say that building professional relationships, networking, and showing up online hasn't been my natural habitat, but I learned and here we are.

And then there's Tall Poppy Syndrome.

One of the harder realities I've faced is that not everyone in the counselling industry supports growth and success. While most people are encouraging and uplifting, there's a minority who seem to take issue with others stepping forward, succeeding, or trying something different. Over time, I've faced criticism and attacks, and while I've learned to develop a thicker skin, let's be honest, it still gets to me sometimes.

What I've come to realise is that it's not really about me at all. It's about their own insecurities, fears, and whatever they're going through in their lives. Some people struggle to see others succeed, and that's their burden, not mine. I won't pretend it's easy. It's an ongoing challenge, and I've had to face my own views of myself and what success means to me. But I've also made peace with the fact that I can't control how others react, I can only control how I show up, lead, and stay true to my own values.

Introduction

The Birth of a Counselling Community

In February 2022, I teamed up with the wonderful Rosie Barbara (my now business partner) and together we founded Counsellors Community Australia, a free Facebook group for Australian counsellors. What started as a simple online space to connect and support each other quickly exploded in growth. As of 2025, we have over 8,000 members, a premium Circle community with 400 members, and run monthly low-cost workshops to support counsellors in their careers. The community has become a core part of my work, and it's been incredible to watch it grow into a movement that empowers and connects Australian counsellors.

Lessons Learned

If I've learned anything, it's this: 'Rome wasn't built in a day.'

I've always been in a bit of a hurry, dreaming up a million ideas and wanting everything done yesterday. But I've come to appreciate pacing myself and staying realistic about what's possible, particularly as I've gotten older.

A tough lesson for me to learn (because I'm fiercely independent) was to know when to get help. I've learned that while you can do everything yourself, you absolutely shouldn't. Support is essential, even if it costs money (yes, you do need to spend money in business).

Finally, stop comparing yourself to others. We're all on the same road—the same journey—but we all started at different times. Sometimes we walk alongside each other, sometimes we pass each other, some of us stop for a break or take a detour and it's all ok! You're exactly where you need to be right now in *your* journey.

Final Thoughts

When I created my business, I had no idea what I was doing. I had never run a business and had always been employed, but I persevered, kept going, pushing through, occasionally falling in a heap, but always getting back up!

I didn't do this *alone*.

Along the way, I've been privileged to support the clients who have trusted me with their stories, pain, triumphs and journeys—I'm truly honoured. It's an incredible thing to be trusted with someone's story and to walk beside them through life's toughest moments. Colleagues I now call friends, those who have stood by me, encouraged me, and held me up during the hardest professional and personal seasons, have been an essential part of my journey. We all need a trusted support system, and I'm deeply grateful for mine.

It's a privilege to be a counsellor. I feel so incredibly blessed to be part of so many counsellors' journeys, and to support them as they navigate the seasons of their counselling careers, just as I've navigated mine.

I started with zero business skills, no financial confidence, and no clue how to run a practice, but I kept learning, adapting, and taking one step at a time. Now, my business is stable, fulfilling, and growing. I'm no one special! I don't possess any superpowers, so if I can develop a successful and sustainable business, so can you if you read on.

Chapter 1

THE COUNSELLOR'S CHAIR: THE FRAMEWORK THAT HOLDS EVERYTHING TOGETHER

A well-built chair does more than just give you a place to sit, it supports you, stabilises you, and allows you to rest while you work. But when a chair is missing a part, when it's wobbly or unbalanced, it becomes uncomfortable. If it's not fixed, eventually, it collapses altogether.

Your private practice is no different.

When I first started developing my *Private Practice Fundamentals* workshop, I kept coming back to the image of a chair, not just any chair, but the kind we, as counsellors, think about a lot. A chair that's warm, inviting, and safe, the space where clients open up, work through their struggles, and experience transformation.

But the more I worked with this idea, the more I realised that the chair wasn't just a symbol of the counselling space, it was the perfect analogy for private practice itself. Every part of a well-built chair represents a different aspect of what holds up a successful counselling business. When everything is strong and working together, your practice feels solid and balanced, but if one piece is missing, weak, or neglected? The whole thing wobbles, and eventually, it falls apart.

I know this firsthand, both in business and in real life.

When the Chair is Unstable, Everything Hurts

I have a pinched nerve in my back, which causes discomfort in my hip, side, and leg. The chairs I sit on directly impact how I function, not just physically, but mentally and emotionally too. If I sit awkwardly or in a poor position, I feel it. The pain lingers. It affects my mood, energy, sleep, and even relationships.

And I see the exact same thing happen to counsellors who try to build a practice without a strong foundation. If your chair, your business, isn't structured well, the strain isn't just felt in your work, it seeps into everything.

- You might feel constantly exhausted, carrying the weight of disorganisation.

- You might be financially stressed, never quite sure when the next client will book in.

- You might find yourself resenting your work, feeling like you're running a business rather than helping people.

- And worst of all? It can impact your self-care, confidence, and longevity in the profession.

This is why every part of the chair matters.

A solid chair needs strong legs, a comfortable seat, a supportive backrest, and well-placed armrests. It also needs wings, because, as counsellors, our work is deeply personal, and self-care isn't a luxury; it's a necessity. Each part of this chair represents something critical in private practice:

1. The Legs – The Foundations of a Private Practice

A chair cannot stand without strong legs, and the same is true for your practice. This foundation keeps everything upright, steady, and functional. Without it, your business is shaky at best and at worst will collapse.

Your four foundational legs are:

- Business Structure: Are you clear on how your business is set up? Sole trader, company, or partnership—what's the best fit for you? Do you understand your obligations?

- Financial Management: Are your finances working *for* you, or do they leave you stressed at the end of each month? Are you charging enough? Do you have systems in place?

- Competence as a Counsellor: No matter how great your business is, if you don't feel confident in your skills, it's going to show; clients notice when we second-guess ourselves.

- Mindset as a Business Owner: Have you truly accepted that you're running a business? Many counsellors resist this, and it holds them back. Private practice is more than just client work, it's about embracing your role as a business owner.

2. The Seat – The Day-to-Day Operations of Your Practice

This is where you sit, the daily rhythm of your work. If your systems, scheduling, and client management aren't organised, you'll constantly feel like you're chasing your tail. Your practice needs to run smoothly so that you aren't stuck dealing with chaos every day.

3. The Backrest – Marketing & Growth

A backrest supports you, just like marketing and visibility support your business. Without a steady flow of clients, you'll be left leaning forward, exhausted, trying to hold everything up on your own. Marketing isn't about selling yourself, it's about letting people know you exist, that you can help them, and making it easy for them to find you.

4. The Armrests – Confidence in Clinical Practice

Your counselling skills, ethics, and professional development provide the structure for you to do the work. When you feel secure in your clinical practice, you can sit comfortably, knowing you're delivering high-quality counselling services.

5. The Wings – Protective and Restorative Self-Care

These wrap around you, offering protection from burnout, vicarious trauma, and the emotional toll of counselling.

The Counsellor's Chair: The Framework That Holds Everything Together

One wing is preventative self-care, setting boundaries, maintaining balance, and proactively protecting your well-being. The other wing is restorative self-care, what you do when you're already depleted and need to recover.

Without both wings in place, you won't be in this industry for long.

The Guide I Wish I Had

I wish someone had come along and told me all of this when I was starting out, without charging me a fortune. I had to figure it out on my own, through trial and error, by making mistakes, and celebrating small wins along the way. I wish I'd had a guide, someone who had already walked the path and could say, 'Here's what you actually need to focus on.'

This book is that guide for you.

Not a quick fix, not a shortcut, but a solid, practical roadmap for building a practice that works. Private practice isn't just about being a great counsellor, it's about building something strong enough to hold you, your clients, and your future.

Your Journey Starts Here

As you move through this book, we'll further break down each part of the Counsellor's Chair, showing you exactly how to build, strengthen, and reinforce each element so that your practice is enjoyable, balanced, sustainable and over time, profitable.

Chapter 2

MEET COUNSELLOR CASEY

As you're reading this book, you've likely pondered what it truly takes to turn a dream of private practice into a reality.

In this chapter, you'll meet Counsellor Casey, a relatable figure whose story will weave through the pages of this book. Casey is at the very beginning of their counselling journey—that happy but scary time! We're going to follow Casey as they travel a path of private practice through the highs and lows, wins and difficult moments. Casey is your guide and also a mirror—helping you to reflect.

Casey's story is designed to engage your emotions, inspire your journey, and offer practical insights into the realities of setting up a private practice. As we explore each element of the Counsellor's Chair framework, you'll see how the lessons from each chapter unfold in Casey's life. Casey will travel with us, navigating the various stages of the framework. This isn't just a theoretical journey, it's a practical one, lived through Casey's relatable ups and downs.

Casey is an entirely fictional character, created as a representation of the collective experiences and insights I've gathered over years of supporting counsellors in establishing their private practices.

Counsellor Casey's Background

At 45, Casey is at a crossroads, ready to leave behind two decades in the corporate world and step into something new. They've always been the one people confide in, the go-to for advice, the steady, compassionate listener. Whether it was colleagues looking for guidance or friends sharing their struggles, Casey naturally fell into the role of supporter. But for years, the idea of turning that into a career never seemed like a real possibility. Life, as it often does, had taken another path, one paved with deadlines, management roles, and the relentless pace of corporate life.

That path, however, began to wear thin. Over the years, the high-pressure environment took its toll. Burnout became an unwelcome companion, and Casey started to feel a deep sense of misalignment with the work. When an organisational restructure came, Casey was offered a redundancy package. While some colleagues saw it as an ending, Casey recognised it as an opportunity, a chance to press pause, reassess priorities, and pursue something meaningful.

It was a deeply personal experience that ultimately confirmed this new direction. Years earlier, Casey had sought counselling after a serious car accident. The support and healing that process provided left a lasting impression. Could counselling be more than just a helping hand for others? Could it become a way of life? With this thought in mind, Casey enrolled in a Bachelor of Counselling and spent the next three years immersing themselves in the theory and practice of what they hoped would become a fulfilling second career.

Graduating was a moment of pride and possibility. With a supportive partner and two children cheering them on, Casey felt a renewed sense of purpose. Financially, the family wasn't in immediate peril, there was some breathing room, and Casey had set aside $10,000 to invest in starting a private practice if it became necessary. But the reality of entering the counselling workforce was harsher than anticipated.

For six months, Casey sent out job applications with growing frustration. Each role seemed to demand a minimum of three years' experience; a catch-22 that left Casey disheartened. How was anyone supposed to gain experience if no one was willing to give them a chance? Volunteering full-time wasn't an option; income would be needed within the next 12 months. And while some contract roles were available, they either required experience or offered pay rates so low that it hardly seemed worth it.

Eventually, Casey landed a part-time case management role in the mental health field. It was a step in the right direction, but it wasn't counselling. The hours were low, just 15 a week, and the pay wasn't great. As time went on, the dream of becoming a full-time counsellor started to feel further and further away. Had they made the right call? After all that time and effort, was this really going to work?

Casey wasn't ready to throw in the towel just yet. Instead of waiting for the ideal job to show up, they decided to take matters into their own hands, starting a private practice while working part-time. Being in a regional area, offering general counselling to the community seemed like the best approach. It was a logical choice, but it didn't come without its challenges.

Having spent their entire career in structured corporate environments, Casey now found themselves in uncharted territory. Running a business felt overwhelming, there were so many decisions to make, and so much to learn. Marketing, in particular, felt intimidating. Although Casey had experience negotiating and building partnerships in the corporate world, promoting a personal business felt different. Vulnerable. Daunting.

In an effort to find guidance, Casey joined an online group for counsellors, hoping for clarity and support. There was some great feedback, but instead of answers, they found themselves drowning in a sea of advice. One person swore by social media marketing, another championed networking, while yet another insisted on focusing solely on SEO (whatever that is!). The sheer volume of information left Casey feeling more confused than ever.

As someone who tended to avoid challenges under pressure, Casey struggled to push through the uncertainty. Self-doubt crept in. Would clients even want to see a beginner counsellor? Would they trust Casey with their most vulnerable moments? The fear of making mistakes, and not knowing how to identify or correct them, weighed heavily. While Casey's partner and friends offered emotional support, the thought of night-time counselling sessions impacting family time added another layer of anxiety.

Casey's perfectionist tendencies often made the road ahead seem even steeper. The idea of failing, of not doing things 'well enough', was a constant shadow. Yet, there was hope. Casey had some savings set aside to get things started, and they believed that with the right approach, there was real potential to make it work. The dream

Meet Counsellor Casey

of a thriving practice, happy clients, steady referrals, and doing meaningful work.

We meet Casey right at the beginning of their counselling career—a time filled with excitement, the possibility of what's around the corner and where this path might take them. Casey is smart, dedicated, hardworking, and has a dream—a vision—but stepping into the unknown comes with plenty of doubts and what-ifs. Their journey is similar to mine and to yours, one that'll hopefully inspire and motivate.

Through the chapters of this book, we'll walk alongside Casey as they explore the foundational elements of private practice. We'll celebrate their wins, learn from their setbacks, and witness the transformation that comes with 'doing the work' and riding the emotional rollercoaster of business. Join Casey as they discover what it takes to build a private practice that's not just successful but also sustainable and, most importantly, enjoyable!

So, let's take a seat in your counsellor's chair and join Casey on this adventure. Their story is just beginning, and so is yours.

Chapter 3

MINDSET & MOMENTUM: THE INVESTMENT THAT POWERS YOUR JOURNEY

*'Whether you think you can, or think you can't –
either way, you're right.'*
Henry Ford

There's a lot that goes into building a private practice—business structures, marketing strategies, and financial planning—but the one thing that underpins it all is mindset. You can have all the right systems in place, the best website, and the perfect therapy room, but if your mindset isn't in the right place, none of it'll work the way you want it to.

I see it time and time again, counsellors stepping into their private practice with a romanticised vision of what it'll be like. You picture a full calendar of eager clients, deep and meaningful sessions, and the freedom of being your own boss. Maybe you imagine walking into a beautiful, well-lit therapy room, sipping coffee between sessions, feeling fulfilled and in control.

Don't get me wrong, having a vision for your desired future is important, but the gap between expectation and reality can be where disillusionment creeps in. Because here's what often happens instead in the early stages of private practice. The phone is quiet. Clients are sporadic. You set up a website, post on social media, maybe even list yourself on directories, and…nothing. You start wondering, *why isn't this working? I've done all the right things. What am I missing?*

This is the point where many counsellors start questioning themselves:

- Maybe I'm not good enough.
- Maybe I should lower my fees.
- Maybe I'm not meant for private practice after all.

And before they've even had a real chance to get their practice off the ground, self-doubt has already convinced them to step back. The truth is, starting a private practice is a long game. Clients don't appear overnight. The key difference between those who push through and succeed and those who burn out and walk away is persistence and realistic expectations.

Fear of Failure – Persistence Over Perfection

One of the biggest misconceptions about private practice is that if you do all the 'right' things, success will follow quickly. I've had

Mindset & Momentum: The Investment That Powers Your Journey

countless counsellors say to me, 'I set up my website, I'm active on social media, I've listed on directories…so where are the clients?'

There's this belief that if you tick all the boxes, have a polished online presence, set up your practice legally, and tell people about your services, clients should start rolling in. And when that doesn't happen straight away, self-doubt kicks in. What am I doing wrong? Why is this working for others but not for me?

Building a reputation, gaining visibility, and developing strong referral pathways takes time. Just because you're not seeing immediate results doesn't mean you're failing, it means you're in the building phase.

The difference between counsellors who succeed and those who give up isn't talent, marketing ability, or even experience. It's persistence plus action. It's the willingness to show up consistently, even when the phone isn't ringing as often as you'd like. It's having the patience to keep refining your approach, learning from what's not working, and trusting that if you stick with it, momentum will come.

That little voice creeps in, *if this was meant to happen, wouldn't it have worked out already?* But business doesn't work that way. Growth is rarely linear, and success is never instant. Every established counsellor I know, including myself, has had moments of frustration, quiet periods, and stretches of doubt. What made the difference wasn't luck or a secret formula; it was the commitment to keep going, to adjust strategies when needed, and to trust that the work being done today will create results down the track.

If you're feeling disheartened, the real question isn't, what if I fail? It's: am I willing to keep going, even when it's slow?

Private practice isn't about getting everything perfect. It's about making thoughtful, strategic choices and trusting that, with persistence, your practice will grow.

Scarcity vs. More than Enough – Shifting Your Perspective

One of the most damaging mindsets in private practice is scarcity thinking, the belief that there aren't enough clients, enough opportunities, or enough room for you in the field. I've seen counsellors hesitate to market themselves because they're worried about competition. They think, *there are already so many counsellors in my area, why would anyone pick me?* They become paralysed by the belief that if someone else is succeeding, it must mean less success for them.

Here's the thing: there are more than enough clients to go around. The demand for counselling is higher than ever, and different clients resonate with different practitioners. Someone might look at your practice and feel an immediate connection to your approach, while another person might be drawn to a different style. That's a good thing.

A more than enough mindset shifts the focus from, 'Will I get clients?' to, 'How do I reach the people who need me?'

It stops you from seeing other counsellors as competitors and instead allows you to focus on what makes you unique.

If you catch yourself thinking, *there aren't enough clients,* reframe it to:

- There are plenty of clients looking for the right fit, how do I show them who I am?

- Instead of worrying about competition, how do I focus on building relationships and referrals?
- How can I clearly share what I do best and how I help clients?

When you shift to, 'There's enough for everyone,' your actions change.

Instead of holding back, you start putting yourself out there. Instead of fearing competition, you see collaboration and connection. Instead of doubting whether you can succeed, you start actively creating that success.

The counsellors who succeed aren't the ones who had a perfect plan or never faced doubts. They're the ones who kept going, kept refining, and refused to quit.

The Business Owner Mindset – Work on It, Not Just in It

The biggest mindset shift you're going to need to make in private practice is realising that being a great counsellor isn't enough. You can have all the training, skills, and passion in the world, but if you don't run your practice like a business, it won't survive, no matter how good you are in the therapy room.

Counsellors step into private practice expecting that clients will just appear because they're qualified, ethical, and passionate about helping people. They assume that if they have great skills, word-of-mouth will take care of everything. The hard truth? It doesn't work that way. Word-of-mouth reputation in private practice takes time to develop. Many counsellors come from employment backgrounds where the structure of the workplace provided everything they needed. Clients were assigned, pay was predictable, admin was handled, and there was no need to think about marketing, bookkeeping, or business strategy. The transition to private practice can feel like stepping into the unknown; suddenly, every decision, success, and challenge rests solely on your shoulders.

It's no wonder so many counsellors struggle with defaulting back to the employee mindset, focusing only on client work and avoiding the uncomfortable reality that they're now running a business. They delay business decisions, keep fees too low, avoid marketing, or simply hope that being a good counsellor will be enough. But if you don't take ownership of your business, you won't have one for long.

This is where the business owner mindset comes in. Running a private practice means wearing two hats, that of the clinician and that of the business owner. If you don't make space for both, your practice will always feel chaotic and unstable.

Michael Gerber, in the *E-Myth*, talks about the importance of working on your business, not just in it. It's a simple but powerful distinction. Working in your business means seeing clients, writing notes, answering emails, and staying caught up in the day-to-day. Working on your business means stepping back, thinking strategically, and making decisions that will shape its future. If you don't make time for the second, you'll feel like you're drowning, and your business will possibly collapse.

I often hear counsellors say they'll work on their business 'when they have time'. But there's always something urgent to do, more emails, more admin, and more clients to book in. Growth doesn't happen by accident. It has to be scheduled, prioritised, and treated as an essential part of your practice.

Some of the most impactful things you can do as a business owner include setting aside time for marketing and visibility, financial planning, reviewing systems, and professional development that enhances your business knowledge, not just clinical skills. These aren't optional extras, they're the backbone of a thriving practice.

One of the best pieces of advice I was ever given was to treat business work like an appointment with a client. You wouldn't cancel a client session because you 'got busy', so don't cancel your business time either. Even a couple of hours a week spent on business development can make a massive difference over time. Making the shift from simply being a counsellor to stepping fully into the role of business owner is what separates those who struggle from those who build practices that are both fulfilling and financially feasible. It doesn't have to be perfect. Just start.

The Investment Mindset – Time, Energy & Money

Developing an investment mindset in private practice is understanding that it's an investment, of time, energy, and money. No matter how much passion you have for helping people, no matter how skilled you are as a counsellor, building and sustaining a private practice requires resources.

Here's the truth many people don't want to hear—starting a business costs money. If you're planning to set up a practice without spending a cent, you're in for a tough time. If you're short on cash, then you'll need to invest significantly more time and energy. There's always a cost; it's just a matter of which resource you're drawing from.

Building a practice that's going to last doesn't happen overnight.

'I've done everything right, set up my website, posted on social media, printed business cards, but I still don't have clients. What am I doing wrong?'

Most of the time, the answer is simple: nothing. You're not doing anything wrong. But private practice is a marathon, not a sprint. It takes time for your name to get out there, for referral pathways to develop, and for people to start trusting and recommending you.

This is where expectations matter. If you're still working full-time or studying and can only dedicate a couple of hours a week to your practice, it's going to take longer to build momentum. If you're transitioning from employment, where clients were handed to you and admin was managed by someone else, it can be a shock to realise just how much work goes into running the business itself.

Many new counsellors get frustrated because they don't see results fast enough and start questioning if they're cut out for private practice. But what you put in is what you get out. It takes consistent effort, stamina, and patience to see growth. Don't give up right before things start to take off.

Money – The Unavoidable Reality

Let's get real, starting a private practice isn't free. It's not just about earning an income; it's about running a business, and businesses come with expenses.

I've seen many counsellors resist spending money on things like supervision, insurance, professional development, or marketing, trying to DIY everything for free. While I completely understand wanting to keep costs low, doing everything the cheapest way possible, it often leads to more stress, mistakes, slower growth, and missed opportunities.

There's a difference between an expense and an investment.

Expenses keep your business running—things like insurance, association memberships, and software subscriptions.

Investments grow your business—things like targeted marketing, business coaching, professional development, and outsourcing admin or tech support.

Where to Spend (And Where to Be Strategic)

You don't need to throw thousands of dollars at your practice in the first six months, but you do need to be smart about where you put your money. Here's where investment truly matters:

- Supervision and Professional Development: Not negotiable! Supervision isn't just a requirement, it keeps you grounded, reflective, and ethical. Professional development keeps your skills relevant and recent and your confidence strong.

- Marketing and Branding: You could be the best counsellor in the world, but if no one knows you exist, your practice won't survive. Being visible matters, and that requires some investment, whether it's a simple website, targeted advertising, or networking.

- Business Support: At some point, you'll need help. Whether it's hiring a VA, a bookkeeper, or a marketing consultant, outsourcing tasks frees you up to focus on what you do best, counselling. The sooner you accept that, the smoother your business will run.

The bottom line? Private practice is a commitment. If you're serious about making it work, you need to be realistic about the investment required. Time, energy, and money—these are the resources that will shape your success. You don't have to invest in all three at once, but no investment equals no business.

Imposter Syndrome – The Uninvited Guest in Private Practice

Let's talk about the 'elephant in the room' the little voice in your head that keeps whispering, *'You're not good enough.'* You know the one. The one that makes you second-guess every decision, overthink every client interaction, and convince yourself that everyone else has this whole private practice thing figured out, except you.

Welcome to imposter syndrome, the unwanted companion of almost every counsellor at some point in their career.

Imposter syndrome isn't just for new counsellors, though it certainly shows up a lot in those early days. It can creep in at every stage of business growth. The first time you see a paying client. The first time you raise your fees. The first time you put your name out there and start marketing your services. That sinking feeling of, *who do I think I am?* doesn't just disappear once you have more experience, it just evolves. Even seasoned counsellors can struggle with thoughts like, *what if I'm not actually helping my clients? Or what if people realise I don't really know what I'm doing?*

Let's be real, private practice makes imposter syndrome worse. When you're employed, you have a job title, an organisation backing you, and colleagues to turn to. But when you step into private practice? It's just you. Suddenly, you're not just a counsellor, you're also a business owner, a marketer, an admin assistant, and a financial manager. That can feel overwhelming, and imposter syndrome thrives in uncertainty.

How Imposter Syndrome Shows Up in Private Practice

If any of this sounds familiar, you're not alone:

- Avoiding putting yourself out there and waiting until you feel *'ready'* (spoiler: what if you never 'feel' ready?).

- Hesitating to raise your fees because you don't think you're worth it.

- Spending hours researching instead of taking action, because what if you get it wrong?

- Convincing yourself that success is just 'luck' and that any day now, people will figure out you're not the real deal.

- Taking on too many clients, too much extra training, too much everything, because deep down, you feel you need to *prove* your worth.

The cycle goes like this: self-doubt creeps in → you feel like you don't know enough → you delay taking action → you procrastinate and find something else to do → you feel even more behind → imposter syndrome grows.

It's exhausting.

The Counsellors Chair

Overcoming Imposter Syndrome – Doing It Anyway

Here's the hard truth: confidence doesn't come first. Action comes first and confidence follows.

You can't *think* your way out of imposter syndrome. You have to *do the thing anyway.*

- Instead of waiting to feel ready, start where you are and trust that you'll grow.

- Instead of obsessing over the 'right' way to do things, accept that mistakes are part of the process and will inevitably happen.

- Instead of worrying about being *good enough,* focus on being present and helping your clients.

Supervision is a game-changer when it comes to battling imposter syndrome. Having a space where you can talk openly about your doubts, get perspective, and be reminded that you're not alone is invaluable. And sometimes, we need to challenge our own thoughts. Newsflash! We can speak horribly to ourselves. You would never say to someone else, 'You're not good enough, you have no idea what you're doing, and you should probably quit,' then why would you say it to yourself?

When You Need Extra Support

Now, feeling self-doubt is normal. Every time you do something new, there will be a learning curve, and discomfort is just part of that—goodness, we would never learn anything new if we didn't experience some level of stress or discomfort! But if imposter syndrome dominates your thoughts and keeps you feeling stuck, it may be time to dig a little deeper.

If self-doubt is making you question your abilities to the point where it's affecting your business, confidence, or mental well-being, then seeking therapy can be a powerful step. Sometimes, these deep-seated beliefs about not being good enough come from experiences far beyond private practice, perhaps from childhood, relationships, education, or past workplaces. Identifying where these patterns come from and working through them can be freeing.

Will imposter syndrome ever go away completely? Probably not. But it won't control you anymore. The goal isn't to eliminate every doubt, it's to not let it stop you.

The Comparison Trap: I'll Have What They're Having

If imposter syndrome had a best friend, it would be 'comparisonitis', that irresistible urge to compare yourself to others and decide you're falling short. It's like sitting at a restaurant and saying, 'I'll have what they're having,' without realising they've been at the table much longer, have a different appetite, and are working with an entirely different budget.

Social media only makes it worse. You see a counsellor posting about a fully booked schedule, another talking about hitting six figures, and a third one launching an online program while you're still trying to finalise your website. Cue the downward spiral *Why am I not there yet? What am I doing wrong? Should I be doing that instead?*

The Counsellors Chair

> '*The good life is a process, not a state of being.
> It is a direction not a destination.*'
> **Carl Rogers**

Chasing 'There' – A Destination That Doesn't Exist

Some counsellors fall into the trap of chasing an imaginary destination, a place where they'll finally feel like they've 'made it'. But let's pause for a second: how do you even measure success?

- Is it having a full calendar of clients?

- Is it making a six-figure income? (And if so, is that revenue or actual take-home profit? Big difference!)

- Is it being recognised as an expert in your niche?

- Or is it just wanting to feel *less stressed* and *more secure* in your business?

More importantly, is what you're chasing actually what YOU want, or just what looks good on someone else?

If you're blindly following what others are doing, you might spend years trying to reach their version of success, only to get there and realise it doesn't even feel fulfilling to you.

The Reality Behind the Hype

Let's talk about those income claims for a moment. You'll see business coaches throwing around statements like:

Mindset & Momentum: The Investment That Powers Your Journey

- 'I made six or seven figures in my private practice!'

- 'I built a wildly profitable business in just a year!'

- 'I scaled my income effortlessly while working part-time!'

But here's what they're not telling you:

- How much of that six-figure revenue is actually profit? (Because gross income means nothing if your expenses are eating it up.)

- Are they running a practice, or making money coaching other practitioners?

- How many hours are they working behind the scenes to sustain it?

- Are they burnt out trying to maintain it?

Success isn't just about the numbers; it's about creating a business that works for YOU.

If you get stuck in the 'I'll have what they're having' mode, you risk chasing someone else's version of success instead of building a practice that actually fits your life and values. The key isn't to measure yourself against someone else's highlight reel but to focus on your own progress.

If you're moving forward, if you're showing up and doing the work, you're exactly where you need to be.

The Counsellors Chair

Tall Poppy Syndrome is Alive and Well – How to Stand Tall Without Getting Cut Down

Success in private practice isn't just about battling your own self-doubt, it's also about navigating how others respond to your growth. In Australia, we have a well-known phenomenon called Tall Poppy Syndrome, the tendency for people to cut down those who rise above the rest. Instead of celebrating the success of other counsellors, there's an underlying current of thinking people who succeed are self-serving in some way. It's not driven by any real issue, just the fact that someone is achieving something.

As counsellors, we work in an industry that thrives on compassion, empathy, and support. You would think this means we're all cheering each other on, right? To be fair, many colleagues are genuinely supportive, happy to see others succeed, and willing to lift one another up. But there are also those who, rather than being inspired by another's success, feel threatened by it. They don't want to see someone else doing better than them, and instead of asking how can I grow, too? They look for ways to discredit, criticise, or even outright attack.

I've experienced this firsthand. Co-founding a community of counsellors has been an incredible privilege, but it has also come with a front-row seat to some of the less flattering aspects of human behaviour. Over the last few years, I've been on the receiving end of personal attacks, both publicly and privately, through messages, emails, and online comments. When you step up, become visible, or create something of value, there will always be people who take issue with it. It can cut to the heart of your own core beliefs, and if you're not careful, it can start to wear you down.

But here's the thing: we don't have to play by those rules.

As professionals, we have an ethical responsibility to conduct ourselves with integrity, both in private and public spaces. The codes of ethics we adhere to, whether through our associations, or other professional bodies, explicitly outline our duty to treat fellow counsellors with respect and to avoid speaking ill of others. That means avoiding gossip, resisting the temptation to bite back or being a keyboard warrior when challenged, and staying professional no matter how others behave.

At the same time, let's not confuse kindness with being a doormat. We can be generous, support others, and celebrate the success of our colleagues, but we can also set boundaries with those who repeatedly act out of jealousy, spite, or competitiveness. Not everyone will behave ethically, but we can choose to and we can surround ourselves with those who genuinely want to see us succeed.

So, stand tall. Do good work. Celebrate others. And don't let those with small minds take up space in your big, bold vision.

Penny's Top Tip – Beware of Bells, Whistles & Shiny Balls

In private practice, it's easy to fall into the trap of thinking that having the best of everything will determine success. The latest software, the perfect website, the most polished branding, it all feels important.

I've seen counsellors delay getting started because they believe they need to have everything in place before they can begin. They tell themselves that once they get the perfect logo, the right practice management system, or the best marketing strategy, things will fall into place. But here's the reality, clients don't book because of a fancy logo or a high-tech scheduling system. They book because they connect with you and believe you can help them.

That's not to say these things don't have value. If something makes your practice easier to run, it's a worthwhile investment. A booking system that saves you time? Fantastic. A branding overhaul that makes you feel more confident. That's great too. But if you're spending hours tweaking things, endlessly researching software, or convincing yourself that the business will only work once everything is 'just right,' you're focusing on the wrong thing. The bells and whistles come later, right now, your priority is getting in front of the people who need your help.

Then there's the 'shiny ball syndrome', something I'm well acquainted with. Whenever I feel overwhelmed, unsure, or stuck, I notice something in the corner of my eye—a shiny, glittery, and very pretty ball. Suddenly, that looks like the direction to go now! A different marketing strategy, a new niche, a fresh training course—it all feels exciting, like movement. But more often than not, it's just a distraction in disguise.

I've caught myself chasing after the shiny ball like an overexcited puppy more times than I can count. It happens when I don't know what to do next, when I start looking at what other people are doing and think, *maybe that's what I should be doing too*. And every single time, it takes me away from the work that actually moves my business forward.

For many counsellors, this shows up when they feel like things aren't working fast enough. They see another practitioner launching a course and think, *maybe I should be running a course*. They notice someone talking about a membership model and wonder if that's the missing piece. Instead of refining what they're already doing, they jump into something new, hoping it will be the shortcut to success.

There will always be another shiny ball to chase; another strategy that looks like the answer. But if you're constantly jumping from one thing to another, you never give yourself the chance to see real results. The most successful counsellors aren't the ones who do the most, they're the ones who focus on what truly matters and don't let distraction pull them away from their path.

So, before you invest in something new, before you change direction or throw money at another solution, stop and ask yourself: is this actually necessary right now, or is this just a distraction from the harder, more important work? The bells and whistles can wait; your business needs you to focus on what actually moves the needle.

A letter from Penny for when you're struggling
(hint read this when you're struggling)

Dear Counsellor,

I see you. I see the doubt creeping in, the frustration bubbling up, the exhaustion that makes you wonder if you've made the right decision. Private practice isn't what you expected, is it? It's harder than you thought. You knew it would take work, but maybe you didn't expect *this* level of uncertainty, this many moments of, 'Am I even cut out for this?'

Let me tell you something, every single counsellor who has built a successful practice has had this exact moment—multiple times. The moment when they felt like throwing in the towel. The moment when they looked at their empty calendar, their bank account, their to-do list, and thought, *maybe I'm not good enough. Maybe this was a mistake.*

But do you know what separates the ones who succeeded from the ones who gave up?

They kept going. They persevered.

Not because they had more talent or confidence or some secret formula for success. Not because they never felt fear. But because they chose to push through the discomfort, to take the next step even when they didn't feel ready, to trust that momentum comes from movement and movement comes from taking action.

Right now, you might be telling yourself:

- I should have more clients by now.
- I don't know what I'm doing.
- Everyone else is succeeding while I'm struggling.
- Maybe I'm not good enough.

And maybe, just maybe, you've also started listening to the voices of others. The well-meaning but misinformed advice from friends who don't get what you do. The dismissive comments from those who think counselling isn't a 'real' business. The subtle (or not so subtle) digs from other professionals who seem to have it all together while you're just trying to stay afloat.

Here's the reality: people will have opinions. Let them. It's just one person's opinion, and it doesn't make it correct.

You don't need permission to build this practice. You don't need validation from those who have never walked your path. And you certainly don't need to justify your success, or your struggles, to anyone.

Private practice isn't an overnight success story. It's a journey, not a destination. The work you put in now, on your marketing, your mindset, your systems, and your skills, might not pay off immediately, but it will pay off if you keep going.

Mindset & Momentum: The Investment That Powers Your Journey

That uncomfortable feeling? That's growth. The fear? That's proof you're stepping into something bigger than where you were before. And the truth is, you're not failing, you're becoming.

So, here's what I want you to do. Take a breath. Take a break if you need to. Cry if you have to. Talk to a trusted person. But do not quit.

Instead:

- Remind yourself why you started.
- Look at how far you've already come.
- Stop comparing your journey to someone else's.
- Take the next right step. Just one.

You can do this. It's not a matter of *if*, it's a matter of when and how you decide to show up for yourself and your business.

So, stand up, shake off the doubt, and get back to it. Your future clients need you. But more importantly, you need you to keep going.

With respect, honesty, and a little kind kick on the rear,

Penny
Your Counselling Companion

How's Counsellor Casey Doing?

Casey sat at their desk, staring at the screen, fingers hovering over the keyboard. They had just finished a call with their supervisor, one that had left them feeling both encouraged and exposed.

'You're doing great,' their supervisor had assured them. 'But you need to start seeing yourself as a professional, not just someone trying to 'figure it out''.

That one sentence had stuck.

Because if Casey was being honest, they still felt like an imposter. The excitement of starting their private practice had quickly been replaced by an uncomfortable feeling, they had no idea if they were *really* ready. Each time they put themselves out there, self-doubt crept in. What if clients didn't find value in their work? What if they weren't as good as other counsellors? What if this whole thing was just a giant mistake?

The fear wasn't just about clients. It was about being visible. Marketing, networking, telling people, *'I'm a counsellor,'* it all felt unnatural, almost like pretending. Scrolling through social media, Casey saw other counsellors posting confidently about their work, sharing insights, and talking about their fully booked practices. Meanwhile, Casey was still trying to figure out how to talk about their practice.

The comparison game was exhausting, but Casey couldn't seem to stop playing it, at first, they tried to drown out the doubts by keeping busy tweaking their website, signing up for webinars, and taking another online course. But something their supervisor had said echoed in their mind: *Are you learning, or are you avoiding?* Ouch!

The truth was, Casey had been hiding behind preparation, convincing themselves that if they just knew one more thing, then they'd be ready. But deep down, they knew there was no perfect moment. No magic level of expertise would erase their fear.

So, they made a decision.

They booked their first networking coffee with another allied health professional, just a casual chat, no pressure. They raised their fees by a small amount, even though part of them wanted to keep them low 'just in case'. And they forced themselves to stop scrolling through other counsellors' success stories and start focusing on their own next step. It wasn't easy. It felt uncomfortable. But it also felt like movement.

A few days later, an email landed in their inbox. A new enquiry. The kind of client Casey actually wanted to work with, someone navigating a career transition, just like Casey had. As they responded to the email, a small shift happened.

Maybe they weren't an imposter after all. Maybe they were just a counsellor at the beginning of something real. For the first time in a while, that thought didn't feel scary. It felt exciting.

Later that week, they brought their doubts to supervision, not just the surface-level concerns, but the real fears sitting underneath. The fear of failing. The fear of being 'found out'. The fear of not being enough.

Their supervisor listened, then asked a simple question: 'What if being a great counsellor isn't about feeling ready, but about showing up anyway?'

Casey sat with that. It wasn't about erasing the doubts. It was about moving forward despite them.

> 'Success is not final, failure is not fatal, it's the courage to continue that counts.'
> Winston Churchill

Chapter 4

SOLID LEGS: THE FOUR FOUNDATIONS OF SUCCESS

'It's not the beauty of a building you should look at; it's the construction of the foundation that will stand the test of time.'
David Allen Coe

Every counsellor who sets out in private practice begins with a dream, a vision of helping others, building something meaningful, and creating a business that aligns with their values. But even the best intentions and brightest dreams can quickly diminish if they're not supported by a strong foundation.

Without the right structures in place, what starts as excitement and purpose can turn into stress, uncertainty, and instability. Building a private practice is like building a chair, if the legs aren't strong, the whole thing wobbles. At first, you might not notice the cracks forming, but over time, the strain of an unsteady foundation will show. If you've ever felt overwhelmed by business decisions, financial stress, or uncertainty about your next steps, it's not because you're not good at what you do, it's because you weren't given the roadmap.

The Strength (or Weakness) of Your Foundations

A thriving private practice isn't built on passion alone, it requires structure, strategy, and sustainability. When your business is built on a wobbly structure, every challenge feels bigger, every decision feels harder, and every setback feels personal. I've seen too many counsellors step into private practice, full of enthusiasm, only to feel lost and overwhelmed within a few months. Some underestimate the business side and find themselves drowning in admin, tax obligations, and financial uncertainty. Others struggle with confidence, unsure if they're doing things 'right' or worried that they're missing crucial steps. Some end up burnt out, broke, or back in employment, feeling like private practice just wasn't for them.

By the time you finish this chapter, you'll understand the four core foundations that will give your practice the strong start it needs. To build a private practice that thrives, you need four essential 'legs' to support it: business structure, financial management, professional competence, and stepping into the role of a business owner. These aren't just abstract concepts; they're the pillars that keep everything steady. When these legs are strong, you can adapt to challenges with confidence rather than scrambling to fix things after they've gone wrong.

Without a clear business structure, things can feel chaotic, making even small decisions overwhelming. Without solid financial systems, income can be all over the place, expenses add up fast, and the stress starts to build. And if you're not confident in your skills, self-doubt creeps in, making you wonder if you're on the right track or if your practice can even last. But if you don't fully step into the business owner mindset, you risk spending more time working in the business as the counsellor and not enough time on the business as the owner.

The biggest risk of neglecting these foundations? Private practice starts to feel harder than it needs to be. The passion that got you started gets buried under stress, and you find yourself constantly wondering if it's all worth it. But here's the good news, you don't have to figure it all out on your own.

In this chapter, we're going to break down each of these four essential legs step by step.

Leg One – Business Structure

Every counsellor starts private practice with a vision of helping people, doing meaningful work, and creating a business that aligns with their values. But without the right structures in place, what starts as excitement can quickly turn into overwhelm, uncertainty, and an increasing pile of admin you never signed up for.

This is where so many counsellors get stuck. No one teaches us the business side of private practice. We're trained to hold space for clients, not to figure out tax structures and business registrations. It's easy to put it off, thinking you'll just 'sort it out later' or assuming you don't need to worry about it yet.

But later is just around the corner.

So, let's get this right from the start because a well-structured practice doesn't just make life easier, it protects you, simplifies things, and gives you a solid foundation to build on.

Choosing the Right Business Structure

In Australia, you must have an Australian Business Number (ABN) to legally operate a business. But before you register, you need to choose a business structure that suits your needs. Here's my first big piece of advice:

Talk to an accountant before you do anything. I'm not an accountant and don't claim to be.

Seriously. This is one of those things you don't want to guess at. Your business structure affects how you pay taxes, how you handle legal liability, and how you set up your finances.

At first, I thought, it's just me, surely, it's simple. I quickly learned that one size doesn't fit all. Some counsellors have multiple income streams, some are in partnerships, and some might even have spouses with businesses that change their financial situation.

I've met counsellors who set up companies way too early thinking it would help them save on tax, only to find out it was costing them more in admin and compliance fees. And I've seen others who stayed sole traders for too long, only realising later that they should have transitioned to a company when their income grew.

Here's the basic rundown of your options:

Solid Legs: The Four Foundations of Success

- Sole Trader: The simplest, most common setup for private practice. Your business is tied to your personal tax file number, and all your earnings are taxed as personal income. It's easy to manage and has low admin costs, but it does mean you personally carry the risk if anything goes wrong. Most counsellors are low risk, we don't rush out and buy properties, we don't need expensive equipment (except ourselves!), and we have insurance. But if you're going to buy a building to have a clinic, then sole trader may not be the best option for you.

- Company (Pty Ltd): A separate legal entity, which means your business and personal finances are distinct. There's more admin and reporting, but it offers more protection, especially if you're working with high-risk clients or plan to grow.

- Partnership: A business shared between two or more people. The partnership lodges a tax return but the profit goes to your personal income. Partnerships work well, until they don't. If you go down this path, make sure you have a legally binding agreement in place from the start.

- Trusts: More complex and usually used for asset protection or tax planning. If you're even considering this, get an accountant involved before making any decisions.

For most counsellors, starting as a sole trader makes the most sense. It's the easiest, cheapest, and most straightforward option. But as your practice grows, your business structure might need to change, and fixing it later is a costly hassle.

Your Business Name Matters

Choosing a business name seems easy until you actually sit down to do it.

Counsellors often want a name that's meaningful to them or a bit unusual but forget that clients need to be able to find you easily. Take a name like Finding Hope, a lovely name, but without words like 'counselling' or 'therapy', they're impossible to find online. Clients don't search for hope on Google. They search for counsellors near me.

So, before you lock in your name, consider:

- Relevance to counselling: Does it make it clear that you're a counselling service?
- Simplicity and spelling: Can clients say it, spell it, and type it into Google without confusion? Avoid quirky spelling of names to be different—you'll be so different no one will find you!
- Length and clarity: A short, memorable name is better than a long, complicated one.
- Futureproofing: Using your personal name (Jane Smith Counselling) is fine until you want to grow. Clients will expect to see you personally, which can make expansion tricky.

Then, before you register it:

- Check availability on ASIC (Australian Securities & Investments Commission).
- Check trademarks on IP Australia.
- Secure your domain name (your website).

Solid Legs: The Four Foundations of Success

I always tell people: secure your domain name and business name registration immediately, even if you're not launching yet. The last thing you want is to fall in love with a name and find out someone else takes it first.

Final Thoughts – Why This Leg Matters

I get it, this part isn't as exciting as working with clients. You didn't become a counsellor to figure out tax structures and domain names.

But this is what allows you to do the work you love.

A well-structured business gives you stability, protection, and clarity. It means you're set up for success from day one, instead of scrambling later when problems arise. And once this is sorted, we can talk about money. Because a business without solid financial management won't survive long-term.

Leg Two: Financial Management – Setting Up for Success

Finances. You either love them, or you'd rather curl up in the corner and pretend they don't exist.

Some people are brilliant with numbers, tracking income, forecasting expenses, and making sense of profit-and-loss statements like it's second nature. Then there are people like me.

When I started private practice, my financial approach was somewhere between avoidance and organised chaos. I was fine with everyday budgeting; I could manage household expenses and budgets. But the moment I had to deal with business finances, tax, or profit margins, my brain checked out. The sight of a profit-and-loss statement made me want to rock in a corner.

So, for a while, I acted like an ostrich (head in the sand and you know what in the air!). I had my private practice income going into the same bank account as my employment wages, which made tracking business expenses a complete nightmare. Everything was blended together, making tax time a stressful mess. I had no idea what I was earning, what I was spending, or whether I was actually making a profit.

It wasn't until I hit breaking point at tax time, spending hours untangling transactions, scrambling to pull together receipts, and feeling totally out of my depth, that I realised something had to change. I needed a system.

If you're just starting out, do yourself a favour: set up your financial foundations from day one and save yourself the headache I had. It doesn't need to be complicated or overwhelming—a simple spreadsheet will work fine for now.

Separate Business Finances – Don't Mix Your Money

One of the biggest mistakes I made early on was not separating my business income from my employment income. It wasn't until about a year in that I finally opened a separate personal account just for my private practice. That was a step in the right direction. Finally, when I registered for GST, I made the switch to a proper business bank account.

Solid Legs: The Four Foundations of Success

Here's why that matters:

- Clarity: When everything is mixed together, it's impossible to see what's actually happening financially in your practice. You might think you're making money, but are you really?

- Tax Time Sanity: If you've ever spent hours digging through old statements and emails, trying to work out what was a personal transaction and what was business, you'll understand why this matters.

- Professionalism: Having a dedicated account for your practice makes you look and feel more like a business owner. It sets the right tone for how you manage your money.

Partnering With an Accountant

I cannot stress this enough—find an accountant who understands small business and service-based industries (your life will be so much easier!). It's a partnership to work together on your business finances and health.

Not all accountants are created equal. Some specialise in big corporations; others focus on retail or product-based businesses. You need someone who understands what it means to run a private practice.

Your accountant will be your go-to person for:

- Helping you choose the right business structure (sole trader, company, trust, etc.).

- Advising on what you can and can't claim at tax time.

- Helping you decide when (or if) to register for GST.

- Guiding you on paying yourself, setting aside tax, and superannuation, and making sure you don't get a nasty ATO surprise.

A good accountant is an investment, not an expense. Shop around, ask for recommendations, and find someone who explains things in a way that makes sense to you.

GST – To Register or To Not Register

One of the most common questions in our community is: 'Do I need to register for GST?'

Here's the deal:

Counsellors in Australia are *not* GST-exempt. We have to charge GST once our practice earns over $75,000 in gross income (not net profit).

So, the question isn't whether you'll need to register, it's when.

Some counsellors register for GST from the start, while others wait until they hit the threshold. There are pros and cons to both:

- Registering early: You can claim back GST on business expenses (but it adds extra admin).

- Waiting until you hit $75,000: Less paperwork early on, but you'll need to be prepared when the time comes.

Solid Legs: The Four Foundations of Success

Either way, know your numbers and talk to your accountant. The ATO expects you to register once you reach $75,000, so keep an eye on your earnings and don't leave it too late.

Taking Payments – Make It Easy for Clients

Your clients need a simple, seamless way to pay you.

The easiest method? Bank transfer. It's free, straightforward, and most clients are happy to pay this way. However, some clients prefer card payments. If you want to offer that option, popular payment platforms include Stripe, PayPal and Square.

Whatever you choose, make sure clients know their options upfront. Clear, simple payment systems reduce stress, for both you and them.

Bookkeeping – Find A System That Works for You

Let's talk about keeping track of your money.

For years, I did things the hard way, scrambling at tax time, hunting for receipts, and manually adding everything to a spreadsheet. I had it in my head that this was easier and safer (not sure what I was thinking). Now? I use Xero. It's not cheap, but it saves me hours of stress and makes BAS, tax, and invoicing so much easier (and my accountant is very happy!).

That said, not everyone needs Xero. Here are some other options:

- Spreadsheets – great for beginners (and free).

- Templates from Etsy – custom-made financial trackers.

- Other accounting software – QuickBooks, MYOB, etc.

Whatever you choose, have a system. Don't just 'figure it out later' (trust me, that's painful).

Business Requires Investment

Let's be real: You can't start a business with zero dollars.

I often see counsellors stepping into private practice with the expectation that they can launch, grow, and sustain a business without any financial investment. I get it, when you're first starting out, it can feel daunting to spend money before you're making any. But the reality is that even the leanest private practice setup requires some initial capital.

I started my practice on a budget, so I completely understand wanting to keep costs down. In the beginning, I did the low-cost version of everything, a basic website, manual invoicing, and spreadsheets instead of accounting software. That worked for a time, but as my practice grew, I had to start investing in better systems to make things easier and more efficient.

Your Initial Investment

One thing many new counsellors don't think about is how much money they actually need to get started. This is where capital investment comes in. Capital investment is the money you put into your business from your personal funds. If you're launching a private practice, you need to ask yourself:

Solid Legs: The Four Foundations of Success

- How much do I need to invest to cover my initial setup costs?

- Do I have savings set aside for business expenses?

- How long can I sustain my practice before it becomes profitable?

For some, that might be a few thousand dollars to get set up with a website, insurance, and software. For others, it might be more significant if they're renting an office space or investing in marketing. Here's the thing, the majority of private practices don't make a full-time income immediately.

Expect a Loss Before You Make a Profit

If there's one thing I want counsellors new to private practice to understand it's this: your practice will likely run at a loss in the first year or two—it all depends on your networks. But if it does, that's normal.

I see so many people get disheartened in their first year because they're not making what they expected. They assume that because they're a great counsellor, the clients will just appear, and their business will instantly be profitable. But that's not how it works.

Most private practices take between two to five years to build up a steady stream of referrals, word-of-mouth clients, and consistent income. In the early stages, you'll have:

- Set-up costs (website, branding, insurance, etc.).

- Ongoing expenses (booking systems, OPD training, supervision, advertising).

- Fluctuating income (some months will be busier than others).

If you go into private practice without a financial buffer, you could find yourself stressed and struggling, which isn't good for you or your clients.

So, what's the solution?

Consider Additional Income Streams

Many counsellors keep working part-time in another role while they build their practice. And honestly, that's a really smart move.

That's exactly what I did. I was still working as a school counsellor when I started my private practice, and that income covered my expenses while my practice grew. It allowed me to invest in the right tools and training without feeling financial pressure to take on too many clients too soon.

For some, that might mean:

- Keeping a part-time or casual role while growing their client base. Even if that work is not counselling-related.

- Taking on contract work (EAP, NDIS, case management).

- Running workshops, supervision, or online programs to bring in additional income.

There's no shame in having multiple income streams while you build your practice. In fact, it's a smart financial decision.

Be Strategic – Plan for Slow Months

Even once you're established, private practice income isn't always consistent. You'll have quiet periods, cancellations, and times when client flow slows down, as well as seasonal fluctuations such as Christmas. If you don't plan for that, it can create unnecessary stress.

This is why budgeting and planning ahead is so important.

- Put money aside during your busy months to cover quieter periods.

- Have a plan for diversifying your income if needed.

- Know your numbers and understand how much you need to earn each month to cover your expenses.

I've learned that when you expect fluctuations and plan accordingly, you can navigate the ups and downs of private practice without stress.

Final Thoughts – Don't Neglect the Finances

I know this part of business isn't the most exciting, but it's one of the most important. If you don't get your financial foundations right, it will catch up with you later.

The purpose of a business isn't just to help people, it's to earn an income and, ultimately, to make a profit. I know that can feel uncomfortable for some counsellors (hand up, I used to avoid thinking about the financial side too). But at the end of the day, if your practice isn't financially viable, you won't be able to keep helping people for long.

Here's something I want you to hear clearly: you are worth it.

Your time is valuable. You worked hard, studied hard, and invested so much into becoming a counsellor. You sacrificed time with family and friends, poured your energy into training, and pushed through the challenges of learning a profession that is both emotionally and mentally demanding. That investment matters.

You deserve to be paid for the work you do.

Money isn't the enemy, it's the heartbeat of an effective, successful business. Taking control of your finances doesn't mean chasing profit at all costs; it means ensuring your practice can thrive, your bills are covered, and you're paid for the important work you do.

So, invest wisely, plan strategically, and give your practice the financial structure it needs to thrive. Your future self (and your stress levels) will thank you for it.

Leg Three – Competent Counselling

There's a responsibility that comes with being a counsellor—the responsibility of competency. Yes, we're great listeners, have a warm presence and display empathy. But it's also about being properly trained, working ethically, staying competent, and taking responsibility for your practice. No matter how passionate you are about helping people or how much lived experience you possess, those alone aren't enough, they have to be backed by professionalism, training, and adherence to ethical guidelines.

I'm super passionate about raising the standard of counselling in Australia. I've seen too many people jump into private practice underprepared, not because they don't care, but because they don't realise the level of responsibility that comes with running a private practice. The stakes are high. Clients trust us with their mental and emotional well-being. They need to know they're in the hands of someone who's competent and able to hold that space properly.

As of 2025, the counselling industry in Australia is still self-regulated, but that doesn't mean there are no standards. While anyone can technically call themselves a 'counsellor,' that doesn't mean they should.

If you're serious about building a private practice, you need to be appropriately qualified with a suitably recognised qualification. This means having at minimum, a diploma, bachelor's degree, graduate diploma, or a Master of Counselling. If you've only completed a short online course or a weekend workshop, you're not a qualified counsellor, and practising without proper training isn't only unethical but could cause harm to clients.

To be crystal clear, a qualification is just the beginning. Competence isn't about getting a certificate and calling it a day. It's about continuously learning, growing, and ensuring you're always working within your limits.

The Role of Counselling Associations – Why Registration Matters

Although counsellors in Australia aren't legally required to register with a professional body like the Australian Counselling Association (ACA) or the Psychotherapy and Counselling Federation of Australia (PACFA), if you want to be recognised as a professional, you absolutely should.

Membership with a peak body provides:

- Professional credibility—many employers and referral sources, including EAP providers and the NDIS, require ACA or PACFA membership.

- A code of ethics and scope of practice that ensures you're working to professional standards.

- Access to insurance, supervision, and continuing professional development (CPD) opportunities.

While registration isn't legally required, working outside of an association means you must comply with your state's Health Workers Code of Conduct. Every state has different regulations, and it's your responsibility to be fully informed and up to date about what applies to you.

Supervision Safety Net

I can't stress this enough, supervision is essential! This theme is deliberately repeated throughout this book.

Throughout my career, I've had many moments of uncertainty, situations where I questioned whether I was making the right ethical choices, where clients presented challenges I hadn't faced before or where I simply needed to process the emotional load of the work. Supervision has provided a space to explore these challenges, reflect, and grow.

Supervision isn't just about meeting the association's requirements, it's one of the most important supports you'll ever have in private practice. It provides guidance, accountability, and a reflective space to process your work. It helps you reflect on your practice, ensure you're operating ethically, and navigate difficult client situations with wisdom and care. Having a regular, trusted supervisor means you have a sounding board, a mentor, and a guide, someone who helps you see things clearly, challenges you when needed, and provides support when things feel overwhelming.

Your supervisor needs to be someone who also understands private practice. Agency-based supervision is not the same as supervision for private practice. You need someone who gets the business side of things as well as the clinical.

You're not required to stick with just one supervisor. If you work in multiple settings or with a variety of client presentations, you may find that having more than one supervisor is beneficial. The key is to find the right fit for your needs.

If you don't have a supervisor, stop reading this book and find one now. This isn't optional.

Ongoing Professional Development

Your qualification isn't the finish line, it's the starting point.

Counselling is a profession that requires continuous learning. Keeping your skills up to date, expanding your knowledge, and staying informed on best practices isn't just about meeting association requirements, it's about ensuring you're providing the best possible service to your clients.

Some counsellors leave their Ongoing Professional Development requirements to the last minute, scrambling to complete workshops just to meet their hours. I've been guilty of this myself from time to time when really busy, but professional development is best intentional.

A structured 12-month Professional Development Plan can help you:

- Identify skills gaps that need improvement.

- Choose training that excites and inspires you, not just what's available at the last minute.

- Ensure you're building on skills and knowledge in a way that matches your goals, client needs and long-term vision of where you see yourself.

Beyond formal training, peer learning and networking can also be valuable, whether through case discussions, study groups, or attending professional events. Staying engaged in learning will keep you sharp, prevent burnout, and ensure your practice continues to grow.

Insurance – Protecting Yourself and Your Clients

If you don't have professional indemnity and public liability insurance *and* you're seeing clients, you're taking a huge risk.

- If a client lodges a complaint or takes legal action, professional indemnity insurance helps safeguard you.

- If a client injures themselves whilst visiting your practice, public liability insurance covers you against those claims.

If you're registered with one of the peak counselling associations, they require you to have insurance, but even if you're not registered, you should never practise without it. Insurance for counsellors in Australia, compared to other industries is incredibly affordable. It's really a minor expense, in contrast to other business costs, and not one you can afford to be without.

Final Thoughts – Competence Is Not a Choice, It Is Your Responsibility

Counselling is more than a profession, it's a privilege. People come to us in their most vulnerable moments, trusting that we're equipped to guide them with skill, integrity, and care. That trust is sacred, and it comes with an enormous responsibility.

This isn't just about ticking boxes. It's about being the kind of counsellor you would want to see if you were the client. Someone who isn't just qualified, but competent. Someone who seeks wisdom, not just knowledge. Someone who understands that ethics and professionalism aren't burdens, they're the very things that make this work meaningful.

It's easy to let things slide. To push supervision to the bottom of the list. To do the bare minimum in professional development. To work beyond our scope because we want to help. But the truth is, competence isn't just about what we know, it's about how we show up. It's about making difficult decisions, knowing where our limit is, and seeking excellence (not perfectionism).

I've been in this industry long enough to see what happens when people don't take this seriously. When they cut corners. When they let fear, ego, or exhaustion guide their decisions instead of ethical principles. The cost isn't just professional, it's human. Clients deserve better. You deserve better.

I believe, with every fibre of my being, that this profession thrives when we hold ourselves to the highest standard. Not because we have to, but because we choose to. Because we care.

Leg Four – Being a Business Owner

You're now stepping into the role beyond the clinician

Being a counsellor and being a business owner are two completely different roles. You were trained to be a counsellor, to support clients, facilitate healing, and work ethically and competently within your profession. But running a private practice is an entirely different skillset, one that most counsellors aren't taught.

This leg of the chair is about stepping into the business owner mindset, which we've already covered in detail in the previous chapter. So rather than repeating what we've already discussed, this section will focus on what it actually means to be a business owner, the shift in perspective required, and the key areas you need to keep front and centre if you want your practice to be successful, profitable, and fulfilling.

Because you're not just a counsellor anymore. You're a business owner. And if you neglect that side of your practice, you'll struggle, burn out, or end up closing your doors.

The Critical Difference: You Are Both the Service and the Business

When you walk into a clothing store, the product sits on a shelf, separate from the staff who sell it. When you go to a café, the coffee is made in the kitchen and brought to your table by a waiter. The product and the delivery of the product are separate.

Solid Legs: The Four Foundations of Success

But in private practice, you're the service and the business.

There's no buffer between you and the business itself. You're both the skilled professional delivering the service and the person responsible for running the entire operation. That's where so many counsellors get caught, stuck in the delivery of the service, forgetting that the business itself needs to be nurtured, structured, and grown.

This is why so many counsellors in private practice struggle. They get so caught up in their client work that they neglect the big picture, and before they know it, their practice feels out of control, disorganised, or financially unstable.

I see this time and time again, and I say this with complete compassion: if you don't learn how to work *on* your business, it'll either control you or you'll lose control of your business, and it'll likely end.

Shifting Perspective for Sustainability

Getting lost in the trees is a common occurrence, stuck in the day-to-day work of counselling and forgetting to take a step back and look at the forest—the business as a whole.

You have to keep shifting your perspective, zooming in to focus on client work, and then zooming out to assess your business structure, systems, marketing, finances, and sustainability.

This is a skill that takes time to develop, but if you don't do it, you'll find yourself constantly reacting rather than strategically growing.

The Reluctant Business Owner – Are You Avoiding Growth?

Many counsellors resist stepping into the business owner role because they never saw themselves as 'business people'. They became counsellors because they wanted to help people, not because they wanted to learn about marketing, pricing, and financial management. Some jump into private practice because they can't get a job.

But here's the reality: if you don't actively develop your business skills, your practice will never reach its full potential.

If business doesn't come naturally to you, that's okay. You don't have to figure everything out overnight, but you do need to embrace learning and be willing to develop the skills that will help your practice thrive.

Pricing – The Emotional Weight of Setting Fees

One of the hardest things for many counsellors is pricing their services appropriately.

We tell ourselves all sorts of stories about pricing, like:

- 'I don't want to charge too much and make counselling inaccessible.'

- 'I'm not experienced enough to charge what others are charging.'

- 'I feel bad asking for money for something that people need.'

But here's the thing, pricing your services too low doesn't just impact you. It impacts your clients and your business as a whole.

If you undercharge, you risk undervaluing your expertise, burning yourself out, and making your business financially unviable over the long-term.

I've seen so many counsellors charge less than they should out of guilt, fear, or a belief that they're 'not worth' higher fees. But you're worth it. You worked hard to get here. You invested in your education. You sacrificed time, energy, and money to become a qualified professional.

And the reality is, clients don't base value on what you think you're worth. They base value on what they believe your service will provide for them.

Think about it, what's the value of helping a client save their marriage? Overcoming anxiety? Navigating grief? These are life-changing outcomes, and yet so many counsellors price themselves according to self-doubt rather than true value.

Balancing Accessibility with Sustainability

Of course, we want to make counselling as accessible as possible. My practice has always been committed to providing affordable, accessible and approachable counselling services. But there's a difference between offering ethical pricing and sacrificing your own livelihood. I live in a rural area and what people are willing to pay is different to the city or more affluent areas (hint: this is where your market research is vital).

Some counsellors use sliding scales, offering reduced fees based on a client's financial situation. While this can be a great option in community settings, it can be challenging to manage in private practice, especially when clients self-report their income, and you have no way of verifying financial hardship.

Other counsellors set aside a limited number of reduced-fee spots, ensuring they can provide affordable services without compromising their overall income. This can be a great way to balance accessibility and sustainability.

But the bottom line? You're running a business, not a charity.

If you feel deeply passionate about supporting disadvantaged communities, consider working part-time in an agency, volunteering some hours or setting up a non-profit initiative. But don't run your private practice as though it's a charity, because the reality is, you won't survive long-term if you can't pay your bills.

Boundaries and Policies – Protecting Your Practice

A sustainable business doesn't just rely on pricing, it also relies on clear policies and boundaries.

- Do you have a cancellation policy?

- Do you require payment upfront?

- How do you handle no-shows or repeated reschedules?

- Will you pursue unpaid invoices or use a debt collector?

These are all questions you need to consider before issues arise. If you don't set clear policies from the start, you'll find yourself constantly chasing payments, losing income due to last-minute cancellations, and feeling resentful about unpaid work.

Set the boundaries first, then apply them with grace and flexibility when needed.

Final Thoughts – Owning Your Role as a Business Owner

Ultimately, private practice is a business and the purpose of a business is to generate income and make a profit.

That doesn't mean profit at the expense of ethics. It doesn't mean overcharging or prioritising money over care. But it does mean recognising that financial sustainability is essential if you want to keep doing this work long-term.

Counselling is a calling, but it's also a profession and professions require structure, boundaries, and sustainability.

So, ask yourself, are you treating your private practice like a real business? Or are you simply hoping it will work out on its own?

Because when you fully step into the role of business owner, everything changes. You stop hoping, and you start building. You stop undervaluing yourself, and you start charging based on value. You stop avoiding the business side, and you start owning it.

The Counsellors Chair

Let's chat about those doubts!

I see you; I can nearly read your mind! Maybe you're thinking, *yep do I really need to worry about all of this now?* Or, *I just want to help people, I'm not a businessperson!*

Maybe numbers make your head spin, or setting up systems feels like an extra burden when you're already juggling so much. I get it.

But here's the thing, avoiding these parts of your practice doesn't make them go away. It just makes them harder to deal with later. You don't want to be scrambling at tax time, struggling to track client enquiries, or realising too late that your pricing isn't covering your expenses.

And what about supervision? *It's expensive—do I need so much of it?* Or, *I'm not seeing any clients yet surely I don't need any.* But supervision isn't just about client consultation—it's so much more; it's about growth, support, accountability, and ethical practice. Even the best counsellors need a space to reflect.

Then there's the classic one: *I'm not cut out for the business side of things.* You don't have to love admin or marketing, but embracing this part of private practice is what allows you to do the work you love, without burning out, undercharging, or constantly stressing about money.

I'm not saying you need to have it all figured out today. But every small step you take now will make future-you breathe a sigh of relief. You've got this. Remember, Rome wasn't built in a day!

Solid Legs: The Four Foundations of Success

How's Counsellor Casey Doing?

Casey sat at the dining table, laptop open, a fresh notebook beside them, and a familiar knot of hesitation tightening in their stomach. They spent weeks researching what it actually took to set up a private practice—business registrations, finances, policies, and supervision—and the sheer volume of decisions felt overwhelming.

It wasn't that they weren't excited, this was the dream, right? But after years in a structured corporate world where decisions were made for them, stepping into private practice felt unsettling. Where was the roadmap? The operating procedures that told them what to do next?

Casey had considered just diving in, getting a few clients and figuring things out as they went. After all, some of the other counsellors in the online groups seemed to be doing that. But every time they thought about winging it, a quiet voice inside warned them: *if you don't set this up properly now, you'll regret it later.*

So, they started small. The first steps were business registration, choosing a name, securing an ABN, and deciding on their structure. A sole trader setup seemed like the best fit for now, but even that decision had come with hours of reading and a call to an accountant.

'Okay,' they muttered to themselves, clicking 'submit' on the registration form. 'One thing done.'

Then came finances. Casey had never considered themselves a numbers person, and the idea of bookkeeping made their head hurt. At first, they were tempted to ignore it, surely, they could sort it out later. But after reading about how quickly tax and expenses could spiral out of control, they forced themselves to take action. A separate business bank account was the first step. Then, after some deliberation, they set up a basic accounting app to track income and expenses, nothing fancy, just enough to stay organised.

I don't need to be a finance expert, they reminded themselves. *I just need to know what's coming in and going out.*

Supervision provided Casey with the reassurance that they weren't alone in this.

'I thought I had to figure everything out by myself,' Casey admitted after their session. 'But having someone to bounce ideas off, to check in with, it's like having a life raft which I know that I really need.'

Slowly, things started to take shape. Their practice wasn't up and running yet, but for the first time, Casey felt like they weren't just guessing. Each step, no matter how small, brought a little more clarity, a little more confidence.

There was still a long way to go, but one thing was certain: Casey was no longer standing at the edge of uncertainty, paralysed by what they didn't know. They were building and for now, that was enough.

Action Steps

1. Business Structure

Make sure your practice ticks all the legal and compliance boxes, register for an ABN, register your business name, get the right insurance, and know your responsibilities when it comes to the requirements of your chosen association. Check codes of ethics and scopes of practice.

2. Finances

Create a basic budget for your practice, listing your expected expenses (e.g., supervision, professional development, or software) and income goals.

3. Competence

Schedule regular supervision sessions and identify one professional development activity to complete in the next six months.

4. Business Owner Mindset

Write down your vision and three specific goals for your practice (e.g., number of clients, income target, or services offered), as well as three business skills you can identify and then work on developing.

'Building a strong foundation you can reach even the most unthinkable heights.'
M.J. Moore

Chapter 5

THE SEAT OF OPERATIONS

*'Every job is a self-portrait of the person who did it.
Autograph your work with excellence.'*
Vince Lombardi

You didn't become a counsellor to spend your days drowning in admin, chasing invoices, and scrambling to stay on top of client bookings, but without solid systems in place, that's exactly what happens. Running a counselling practice without a strong seat of operations is like balancing on a broken chair.

Counsellors need a solid base to support their private practice. Otherwise, instability causes a shifting of position to keep things from falling apart. Juggling admin tasks, poor pricing models, chasing invoices, and managing bookings with no clear system. The chaos seeps into your confidence, leaving you doubting your ability to hold it all together. Clients may notice the cracks too, as missed details and disorganisation erode their trust. Over time, the instability can leave you exhausted, questioning your dream, and wondering if private practice is even the right fit for you.

But when your daily operations are sorted, everything changes. You're not playing constant catch-up, you feel like you have some level of control, and your day seems more organised. This reassures your clients that you're reliable and professional which ultimately increases their trust in you. Getting your systems in place also gives you your time back, so instead of drowning in admin, you can actually enjoy a cup of tea or spend quality time with family without feeling like there's always something hanging over your head.

In this chapter, we're going to cover exactly how to get your operations running smoothly so your practice feels calm and in control, rather than chaotic and overwhelming.

First, you'll learn how to create a space that's uniquely yours, yet professional. Whether you're working from a physical office, virtually or even on the road, your work environment matters, so that you and your clients feel comfortable.

Then we'll look at admin without the headaches. From client bookings to invoicing and keeping client records secure, we'll look at simple ways to streamline your admin so you're not constantly chasing your tail. A little organisation goes a long way toward saving your sanity.

Finally, we cover pricing and ensuring that what you're charging is profitable. Discovering a pricing model that suits you, your clients, and your business is the key to ongoing growth. We'll explore how to price in a way that reflects your worth, supports your financial goals, and ensures sustainability.

The Seat of Operations

By the end of this chapter, you'll have practical, realistic strategies to keep your practice running smoothly so you can feel confident in how you manage your business, instead of feeling like you're constantly trying to stay afloat.

Choosing Your Delivery Model

Before anything else, you need to decide how you're delivering your counselling services. There are multiple ways to work with clients, and each comes with its own considerations.

Are you setting up an in-person practice? If so, where will you see clients? Renting a room is an option, but costs vary drastically depending on location. In smaller towns, you might find an affordable community space or shared practice, while city-based rooms can be significantly more expensive. You also need to think about accessibility, privacy, and how clients will enter and exit without crossing paths with others.

Perhaps you're drawn to online counselling, which has grown in popularity. But running sessions over videoconferencing isn't as simple as logging on and chatting. You need to consider your internet connection, video and audio quality, and the security of your digital platforms. Online sessions should feel just as professional as in-person work, clients shouldn't be distracted or disconnected by bad lighting, a cluttered background, or a poor connection that cuts out mid-session.

Other models include walk-and-talk therapy, where sessions take place outdoors, home visits, where you travel to clients, or a mobile practice, where you rotate between different locations. Some counsellors also work from home, setting up a dedicated space within their house. If you go down this path, think about separating your home and work life—having a separate entrance or ensuring a high level of privacy and safety is crucial.

There's also the option of a hybrid model, combining different delivery methods. For example, you might offer in-person sessions two days a week while working online for the rest. Whatever you choose, it's important to look at safety for yourself and the client, work safety processes (if in-person), risk assessments and hazard checks if engaging in home visits or walk-and-talk. Most importantly, check with your insurer and update them on what you're doing so you have sufficient coverage. In the event of an incident, insurance surprises aren't the pleasant kind.

Creating Systems That Work for You

When you first start out, you wear every hat in the business—counsellor, admin assistant, bookkeeper, and tech support. It can feel like a lot, and if you don't put systems in place, things can quickly become overwhelming. The key is efficiency.

You don't need a fancy, expensive system from day one, but you do need some structure. Simple things like a consistent booking process, clear client records, and a streamlined invoicing system make a massive difference. Some counsellors start with free tools like Google Calendar for scheduling and spreadsheets for bookkeeping and manual invoicing. Others prefer all-in-one systems like Splose, Halaxy, or Zanda (formerly Powerdiary), which integrate bookings, payments, and client records into one platform. There's no right or wrong choice—it's about what fits your stage of business and budget.

Email communication is another area that requires structure and efficiency. It's easy to let client emails pile up, responding at all hours of the day, but setting clear policies around response times and expectations prevents admin from taking over your life.

Privacy and security also need to be front of mind. If you're storing client records digitally, make sure you're using a secure system that complies with Australian privacy laws. If you're taking notes by hand, they need to be locked away safely. Many counsellors assume data breaches won't happen to them, but poor security can put both you and your clients at risk.

Privacy vs. Confidentiality

It's important to understand the difference between privacy and confidentiality, as well as where they overlap. Privacy is covered by Australian legislation (Privacy Act 1988), which means there are legal requirements around how client information—particularly personal and health information—is collected, stored, and shared. Confidentiality isn't just a guideline, it's a professional and ethical obligation, backed by common law. Breaking it can have serious consequences, including legal action or professional disciplinary measures. While not every confidentiality breach is a privacy breach, if you disclose a client's personal information without consent (or without a legal requirement to do so, like mandatory reporting), you could be breaching both privacy laws and confidentiality obligations.

For example, sharing a client's mental health condition with a third party without consent? That could be a breach of both. But casually mentioning a session scenario (without identifying details) might not violate privacy law, though it could still be considered a breach of confidentiality and professional ethics. Please consult a lawyer or your association if in doubt about the differences or your obligations.

Every counsellor must have a publicly available privacy policy, outlining how client information is stored and handled. If you're using third-party software, read their policies carefully—you're responsible for ensuring your client data is protected.

Beyond privacy, there are other legal responsibilities to stay on top of. Do you need a working with children check? Are you required to report concerns of abuse or neglect? Are you working with vulnerable people or the elderly? How will you respond if you receive a subpoena for client notes? These aren't things to leave until later—getting clear on your legal obligations early on prevents problems down the track.

Pricing That Reflects Your Value

Pricing is a major sticking point for many counsellors. Why? Because counsellors tend to base fees on what they think they're worth rather than the value of the service provided to the client. Clients don't pay for your self-worth—they pay for the perceived value of counselling in their lives. If someone is struggling in their relationship, the cost of therapy isn't just about the session itself, it's about what they stand to gain, whether that's saving their marriage, improving their mental health, or rebuilding confidence.

At the same time, pricing has to be realistic and sustainable. People value what they pay for, which is why free counselling does have its issues. If your prices are too low, people will question your credibility. If they're too high, you'll outprice some people. It's important to strike a balance that allows you to serve clients while maintaining a profitable business.

There are different ways to structure pricing:

- Flat rate fees: A clear hourly rate.
- Tiered pricing: Offering different session lengths or service types at varying rates.
- Packages: Bundling multiple sessions together, though this requires clear refund policies to comply with consumer laws.

Sliding scale pricing is another option, though I personally don't recommend it. Unlike not-for-profits or government-funded services, we can't 'means test' clients to verify income levels. Offering reduced rates should be done strategically, not as a default. If you feel strongly about making counselling accessible, consider setting aside a limited number of low-cost spots, rather than under-pricing yourself across the board.

A Streamlined Practice = Good Client Care = A Sustainable Future

Operations might not be the most exciting aspect of private practice, but it keeps your business on track and functioning. Without the right systems in place, it's easy to feel like you're always scrambling, overwhelmed, and unsure if you're meeting all your responsibilities. A professional, well-run practice isn't just about admin—it's about creating stability for the long term so that you can show up for your clients with confidence.

By choosing a clear delivery model, implementing systems that work for you, setting legal foundations, and pricing your services appropriately, you're building a business that can grow without burning you out.

Because at the end of the day, a well-run practice doesn't just benefit you—it ensures your clients receive the best possible experience, too.

The Counsellors Chair

Let's chat about those doubts!

I see the hesitation and doubts creeping in. *Do I really have time for this? Can't I just figure it out as I go? I'm not good with tech. I don't want to overcharge. Do I really need all these systems?*

You're not alone in these thoughts. Every counsellor stepping into private practice has felt that same pushback, that same urge to put things off and focus just on the clients.

But here's the thing, without systems, structure, and boundaries, the stress will creep in. The late nights catching up on admin, the endless hours lost to disorganisation, the slow erosion of your energy as you try to do it all manually.

And pricing? If you don't charge for profit, you'll find yourself overworked, exhausted, and questioning if private practice was the right move at all. I know it's uncomfortable. It's hard to step into the business side of things when all you want to do is help people. But running a practice isn't just about passion—it's about making sure you can keep doing what you love without drowning in stress.

You don't have to overhaul everything overnight. One system at a time. One decision at a time. One step at a time. The doubts will always be there, whispering that you're not ready, that it's too much, that you're not cut out for this. But here's the truth: you are. And future you? The one who isn't constantly scrambling, who feels organised, confident, and in control? They're going to thank you for starting today. You've got this, you really do!

The Seat of Operations

How's Counsellor Casey Going?

At first, Casey thought the hardest part of private practice would be finding clients. But as the weeks went by, they realised the real challenge wasn't the therapy—it was everything around it. The never-ending admin, the emails piling up, the scattered bookings, and the awkwardness of chasing payments. They'd ended most days feeling drained—not from sessions, but from trying to keep up.

'I thought I was doing okay,' Casey reflected. 'I had a notebook for appointments, a basic invoice template, and a locked filing cabinet for notes. It felt simple. But in reality? It was chaos.'

The cracks started showing quickly. Clients were getting confused about appointment times. Casey had panicked about an email that went missing and accidentally double-booking themselves. Invoicing was a struggle and a mess and trying to keep track of everything was mentally exhausting. It wasn't just frustrating, it couldn't go on like this.

Still, Casey resisted making changes. 'I kept telling myself, I don't have time to set up new systems or I'll get to it later.'

Later didn't seem to arrive and the stress kept building. Then the last straw—an email system glitch that caused lost documents! Casey was at their wit's end and completely fed up.

The first step was the hardest—choosing a proper booking system. 'I kept putting it off, thinking it was too complicated, and I didn't have time to set it up. But once I made the decision and got on with it, I couldn't believe the freedom and relief it provided. Double bookings stopped and there were no more accidentally deleted forms. I felt a lot more confident in what I was doing.'

Next came payments. The back-and-forth of invoicing, reminding, and following up was draining Casey's energy and confidence. 'Chasing payments made me so uncomfortable—it's like therapy and payment are opposite concepts! However, I realised I wasn't running a hobby, I was running a business. My booking system was a miracle, everything just got sent with a couple of clicks.'

Then, there was the pricing. This was the part that Casey wrestled with the most. 'I kept worrying—what if clients can't afford me? What if I'm asking too much? The guilt was real. But when I really stepped back and looked at the bigger picture—the time spent preparing, the admin and the ongoing costs—I realised that setting the right fees wasn't about being greedy. It was about making my practice viable. Raising my rates wasn't easy, but it was necessary.'

Now? Casey's practice finally feels steady. There's a rhythm to the days, a flow to the work. Admin no longer creeps into every spare moment, and clients move through their systems with ease. It's not perfect—nothing ever is—but Casey no longer feels like they're just holding it all together.

'I wish I hadn't put this off,' Casey admits. 'I thought I was keeping things simple to save money, but really, I just made life harder for myself. Now, everything feels more organised, and I feel in control.'

Their advice for anyone just starting out? 'Sort things out before you're drowning. You don't have to do it all at once—just start with one system, one small change. It's worth it. And trust me, you'll be glad you did.'

The Seat of Operations

Action Steps

1. Set Up a Simple Booking System

Search for a simple, easy-to-use booking system that fits your budget and needs. The aim here is to save your precious time by cutting down on admin and making it easier for clients to book (taking you out of the process, so you can spend more time focusing on what you do best).

2. Create Clear Boundaries and Policies

Create your cancellation, rescheduling, and payment policies and add them to your agreements. Get your supervisor to check if you're not sure. Let clients know what to expect so there's no confusion later. Clear boundaries not only build trust but also protect your time and energy.

3. Carve Out Admin Time in Your Schedule

Book specific blocks of time each week for admin tasks like invoicing, emails, and planning. Treat these blocks like client sessions—they're just as important for keeping your practice running smoothly.

4. Review Client Communication Tools

Think about the journey your clients take from first contact to their sessions. Look at how you communicate: emails, text reminders, and follow-ups, and how you could improve the process, like automating your appointment reminders or using email templates for common messages.

5. Price for Profit

Time to assess your pricing strategy—does it reflect the true value of your skills, time and training, or are you undercharging out of self-doubt? Are your fees covering your costs and allowing for consistent growth, or are you barely breaking even?

'Nothing will work unless you do.'
— Maya Angelou

Chapter 6

MARKETING BACKREST — SUPPORT FOR BUSINESS GROWTH

'Doing business without advertising is like winking at a girl in the dark. You know what you are doing, but nobody else does.'
Stuart H. Britt

You've set up your dream counselling space, ready to make a difference, but no one is booking. Crickets! A practice no one knows about isn't a business; it's just an expensive hobby.

When marketing is done well, it increases your confidence and creates a stable business, one that's viable for the long term. Instead of wondering where your next client is coming from, you'll have a flow of enquiries that keep your calendar steady—without relying on luck or last-minute scrambling. But marketing isn't just about getting people through the door, it's about attracting the right clients. When your branding and messaging are clear, you naturally connect with the people who need your services most, leading to better outcomes for both you and your clients.

A strong marketing foundation allows your business to grow in a way that aligns with your values, capacity, and long-term vision without running yourself into the ground. Instead of throwing spaghetti at the wall and hoping something sticks, you'll have effective strategies that work for you, making marketing easier and less time-consuming. When your marketing is structured and intentional, you avoid the feast-or-famine cycle, allowing you to focus on what you do best—counselling. Over time, your reputation begins to do some of the work for you, through word-of-mouth, referrals, and a strong online presence.

Without a solid marketing strategy, you're leaving your practice's success up to chance. Instead of regular new clients, you'll find yourself constantly wondering, *where are they?*

You'll be left hoping for referrals, waiting for enquiries, and stressing when the phone stays silent. Even when clients do come, they might not be the right fit, leaving you feeling drained and questioning whether private practice was the right move. Worse, potential clients might not even know you exist or they might choose someone else simply because that counsellor has a stronger online presence or shows up first in a Google search.

Financially, the impact is real. No marketing means unpredictable income, financial stress, and feeling stuck in survival mode. Instead of running a steady, thriving practice, you're stuck in a cycle of ups

Marketing Backrest – Support for Business Growth

and downs, never quite sure if you'll have enough clients next month to pay the bills.

Then there's the emotional cost. When marketing is an afterthought, private practice feels harder than it needs to be. The self-doubt creeps in, frustration builds, and energy wanes. You start questioning, *is this actually going to work—did I make the wrong decision?*

In this chapter, we're diving into the marketing backrest—the solid support your business needs to grow and thrive. Because here's the thing: private practice isn't Field of Dreams. Just because you build it, doesn't mean clients will magically appear. Marketing isn't about being pushy or gimmicky, it's about making it easy for the right people to find and choose you.

In this chapter, there are eight sections breaking down the essentials of marketing your private practice so you can attract the right clients without feeling like you're shouting into the void. We'll start by getting clear on who you're trying to reach because if you try to market to everyone, you'll connect with no one. Identifying your ideal clients and positioning yourself effectively is the foundation of any strong marketing strategy. From there, we'll explore branding and messaging—not just logos and visuals, but how to build trust, connection, and recognition.

Marketing takes time, and not all strategies work the same way. Some, like SEO and referrals, build results gradually, while others, like ads and promotions, can bring in clients more quickly. Knowing when and how to use each will help you create a plan that works both now and in the long run. Referrals are one of the best ways to grow a practice, but they don't just happen—you need to be intentional about building strong professional relationships that generate steady client enquiries.

Your online presence matters, but it doesn't have to be overwhelming. We'll focus on the most important bits: what makes a website work, how to help clients find you easily, and how to use social media without it taking over your life or making you feel like you have to do the latest TikTok dance craze! The goal isn't to be everywhere online or tweaking your website non-stop but to help clients find you in a way that is effective and authentic.

Section One: Identifying Your Ideal Client

A common trap many counsellors fall into—especially in the early days—is trying to appeal to everyone. I get it. You want to help as many people as possible, and saying yes to any client who walks through the door feels like the safest and most helpful way to build your practice. But, if you try to be for everyone, you become forgettable to everyone.

When you aren't clear about who you serve, your marketing becomes scattered, your messaging feels bland, and you end up attracting clients who may not align with your strengths or passion. That's how burnout creeps in—when you spend too much time working with people whose needs, issues, or energy drain you rather than energise you.

So, how do you figure out who your ideal client is?

Let's take a step back. Instead of trying to cast a net into the entire ocean or focusing only on where the need is, start with *you*.

Who are the clients you genuinely enjoy working with? The ones who leave you feeling energised rather than drained?

Marketing Backrest – Support for Business Growth

Your ideal client isn't just about a demographic—it's about connection. It's the type of person who fits your skills, interests, and counselling style. Ask yourself:

- What issues are you most passionate about supporting clients through?
- What kinds of client stories, personalities, or challenges do you naturally connect with?
- Are there common threads among the clients you've enjoyed working with the most?
- What gives you a sense of joy in your work? To figure this out, do the joy versus dread test. Visualise the clients or issues you're thinking about working with. Picture yourself waking up in the morning and seeing your schedule for the day. Does that client issue fill you with a sense of joy or dread? If it's joy, great! If it's dread, set aside time to reflect.

Once you've got a clearer picture, you can start refining it further. A useful tool here is creating a client avatar or case study (in counselling terms)—a detailed representation of your ideal client. This includes both demographics (age, gender, location, relationship status) and psychographics (emotions, values, beliefs, pain points, fears, and goals).

For example, rather than saying, 'I work with women who have anxiety,' you might refine that to, 'I support women in high-pressure careers who struggle with anxiety and imposter syndrome, helping them manage stress, set boundaries, and regain confidence.'

This level of clarity changes everything. It sharpens your marketing, refines your messaging, and makes it easier for the right clients to find you. But here's where people get stuck fearing that niching down will limit their opportunities. The worry sounds something like this: 'If I get too specific, won't I miss out on potential clients?'

The opposite is true. When you market to everyone—you market to no-one. When you speak directly to a specific group, people feel seen, they feel you understand their struggles and that's what gets them to reach out to you. Of course, this isn't about rigidly boxing yourself in either. Clients outside your ideal niche will still reach out, and you can decide whether to work with them. But by having clarity on who you want to serve, you attract more of the right people rather than taking on anyone just to fill your calendar.

Once you have a rough picture of your ideal client, the next step is to test it through conversations, research, and refining as you go. This process isn't about locking yourself into a single client profile forever. It's about giving your marketing focus so you can build a practice that you love—one that fills you with joy. Remember, your private practice is building something that reflects your vision and values, not just creating an income.

Section Two: Market Research

Once you've identified your ideal client, it's vital to conduct market research. This is where eyes can glaze over and counsellors either skip ahead too quickly, feel it's boring (which it can be), jump straight into marketing without a strategy, or feel completely overwhelmed by where to even start and don't do it.

Why Market Research Matters

Before you invest in branding, websites, or advertising, you need to understand the demand for your services, the competition in your area, and the gaps that exist. This isn't just about location—it's about looking at the services already available, their pricing structures, their referral sources, and the clients they attract. It's also about understanding whether the market is already saturated and, if so, how you stand out.

Imagine opening a practice in an area where multiple well-established counsellors are already offering the exact same services as you. If there's no clear point of difference, it'll be much harder to gain traction. However, if you find an under-served niche within that space, you can carve out a position for yourself more effectively. For example, there might be many general relationship counsellors in your area, but very few who specialise in supporting blended families, neurodiverse couples, or FIFO relationships.

How to Conduct Effective Market Research

Start by researching your geographic area (or the online space if you plan to work remotely). Look at:

- Existing counsellors, psychologists, and social workers: Who are the key players? What services do they offer? How do they present themselves?
- Agencies, government-funded services, and non-profits: Are there organisations offering free or subsidised services in the areas you want to work in? If so, are they attracting the same clients you're hoping to work with?
- Referral partners: Who are the people likely to refer to you? GPs, allied health professionals, community centres, schools, gyms, or even alternative therapists? What gaps exist in these networks?

Finding Your Unique Position in the Market

One of the most valuable parts of market research is finding what's missing. If you're new in the market, you're competing with well-established counsellors and it's hard to make your mark. Finding a point of difference or a gap in the market is vital. What's your unique value? Maybe it's the way you work, your lived experience, a specific modality you use, or the way you structure your sessions.

For example, perhaps you want to work with couples, but there are a few counsellors already offering general counselling in this space. You have lived experience around divorce and decide to focus on divorce-recovery and life after divorce.

The Importance of Flexibility

Market research isn't something you do once and forget. The counselling industry, like any business, shifts over time. New competitors emerge, client needs change, and your own interests and skills evolve. Your initial research gives you a strong foundation, but you should revisit it regularly, especially if you're struggling to attract the right clients. Hopefully, the result is you'll have a clear, intentional approach that puts you in front of the right people, particularly those who genuinely need and value what you offer.

Section Three: To Niche or Not to Niche – That Is the Question!

Many counsellors hesitate when it comes to niching, as they're worried about limiting their options or unsure of how to define their focus without boxing themselves in. Many counsellors resist defining a niche because they worry it will limit their opportunities, cutting them off from potential clients. Others feel pressure to specialise immediately, believing they need a mountain of advanced training to be taken seriously. But niching and specialisation are not the same thing.

Niching vs. Specialisation: What's the Difference?

The term specialisation comes from the medical model. If you needed a knee replacement, you wouldn't go to your GP, you'd see an orthopaedic surgeon. That's because a specialist has deeper training and experience in a particular field—the result would be disastrous if you got your GP to give you a new knee! In counselling, specialisation works the same way. A specialist has advanced, targeted expertise, often backed by additional formal education and extensive hands-on experience.

Niching, however, is about clarity. A niche defines who you work with or the key issue you help with, of course, within your scope of practice! It's about being clear on who you serve and why they should choose you.

For example, let's say you want to work in the area of addiction. You could:

- Niche in working with women experiencing behavioural addictions

- Specialise in motivational interviewing or addiction-specific trauma therapy

One defines who you help, the other defines how you help them. It can also be both.

A niche might be based on demographics (e.g., first responders), life experiences (e.g., divorce recovery), or a specific topic (e.g., relationships). It's not about limiting yourself, it's about making it easier for the right clients to find you.

Why Niching Makes Private Practice Easier (Not Harder)

Counsellors new to private practice often think that seeing everyone or being a 'generalist' will bring in more clients, but it often does the opposite. It can make it harder to attract the right clients and even take the joy out of the work. Clients don't necessarily search for a 'counsellor'—they search for someone who understands their specific problem.

Think about it: if a woman in a high-pressure corporate job is experiencing burnout, is she more likely to book with:

1. A generalist: 'I offer counselling for all adults dealing with stress, anxiety, and life transitions.'

2. A niche counsellor: 'I help women in corporate careers manage stress and prevent burnout while maintaining work-life balance.'

The niche-focused counsellor is most likely to attract that client because they immediately speak to the client's struggle and position themselves as the right fit.

Niching doesn't mean you can't see other clients, it just means you have a clear message that makes it easier for your ideal clients to connect with you.

Specialising – When and How to Do It Ethically

You should only call yourself a specialist if you have advanced training and years of experience working in that space. Calling yourself a specialist without the proper qualifications can mislead clients, damage your credibility and potentially lead to ethical breaches.

Not every counsellor needs to specialise, but every counsellor can benefit from some level of niching. If you skip this step, you'll struggle to stand out in a crowded industry. The more intentional you are about how you position yourself, the easier it becomes to attract clients who connect with your message.

Section 4: Creating Your Unique Selling Proposition (USP)

Your Unique Selling Proposition (USP) is what sets you apart in a crowded industry. Counselling is a deeply personal service, and clients are often choosing between multiple professionals who offer similar support. Your USP helps them understand why you're the right fit. It's not about claiming to be the *best*—it's about clearly communicating what makes your practice different from the next counsellor down the road.

A strong USP follows a simple formula:

Service/Service provider + Target Market + Benefit

For example:

'I provide person-centred counselling for young adults navigating life transitions, helping them gain clarity, direction, and a sense of purpose.'

This communicates what you do, who you help, and the benefit of working with you - but what makes it unique? That's where your point of difference comes in. Maybe it's your lived experience, your style and approach, or a specific modality. It could even be the way you make therapy feel more accessible, practical, or engaging.

Your USP isn't just a sentence for your website—it's the foundation of all your messaging. It should shape how you market your services, introduce yourself at networking events, and position your business. If you can't clearly explain why clients should choose you, neither can they.

If you're struggling to refine your USP, AI tools like ChatGPT can help generate different versions based on your input. Just be sure to tweak the wording so it feels authentic to you.

Once you've nailed it, use your USP everywhere—your website, social media, and networking conversations. The clearer and more specific your positioning, the easier it will be for the right clients to find you. It's often called an elevator pitch, something you can explain to people when you are going up in the elevator. You don't get long so make it count!

Section Five: Building Your Brand Identity

Branding. Some counsellors love graphic designing and immersing themself in a world of colour and creativity (I do). But it's a word that can make others feel uneasy and pressured, bringing to mind flashy logos, pushy marketing and going down the black hole of graphic design software. But really, branding isn't about trying to stand out for the sake of it—it's about making it easier for the right clients to find you, trust you, and feel confident reaching out.

In private practice, your brand identity is how people experience you before they ever book a session. It's the way your website makes them feel, the voice in your emails, the message behind your services, and the way you speak on the phone. It's what helps clients decide, yes, this is the counsellor for me.

The Story Behind Your Practice

Why did you become a counsellor? What drew you to this work? What do you believe about healing, change, and personal growth?

For some, the story is deeply personal—perhaps they've overcome struggles similar to their clients, or they've worked in an industry that gives them unique insight into a client's world. Others may not have a personal connection to their niche but bring a strong professional philosophy or therapeutic approach that sets them apart.

There's no one way to craft your brand story. Some counsellors weave their personal experiences into their practice, while others keep the focus on their skills and approach. Sure, there are templates available online to help you do this but it's about being genuine and finding the balance between personal and professional that feels right for you.

If you're not sure where to start, ask yourself:

- What do I believe about the counselling process?

- How do I want my clients to feel when they work with me?

- What values shape the way I practice?

- What sets me apart from other counsellors?

Bringing Your Brand to Life

Once you've shaped your brand identity, the next step is translating that into a cohesive, professional presence. This isn't just about making things 'look nice'—it's about consistency. Clients feel safer with predictability, they want to know what to expect when working with you. That's why everything from your website to your emails, your business cards to your intake forms, should carry the same tone, message, and feel.

Colours, fonts, and logos matter but only in the way they reinforce your brand's personality, making intentional and thoughtful choices that represent the emotion and energy of your practice.

Consistency: More Than Just Looking Pretty

Your brand doesn't just live on your website—it's in every touchpoint a client has with you. A professional, welcoming website means little if your email responses feel cold or rushed. A calming therapy space loses its impact if your intake forms are confusing and impersonal. Every detail, no matter how small, contributes to the way clients experience you.

Branding is also about alignment. If your website talks about supporting client well-being but your schedule is chaotic, or your Instagram presence is polished but your emails are abrupt, clients will sense the inconsistency. Your brand should be an honest reflection of what it's actually like to work with you.

Why Branding Makes You Stand Out

In a sea of counsellors offering similar services, strong branding helps you stand out, not by being the loudest, but by being the clearest. It's not about trying to 'sell' yourself, it's about making it obvious why the right clients should choose you.

Branding isn't a marketing 'gimmick', it's what makes your practice feel purposeful, professional, and uniquely yours.

Section Six: Quick versus Slow Marketing Strategies

Hopefully, by now, you've done your action steps. You've defined your niche(s), identified your ideal client, crafted your unique selling proposition (USP), and created your unique brand story. If you haven't, stop here and go back. Skipping these foundational business steps and jumping straight into marketing is a rapid way to waste time, energy, and money. It's frustrating when counsellors pour resources into ads, social media posts, or networking efforts, only to hear nothing.

Marketing isn't about throwing everything at the wall and hoping something sticks. It's about making sure the right people—your ideal clients—find you, trust you, and take action. This is where quick-response and long-term marketing strategies come in. Each serves a different purpose, and a successful private practice needs the wise application of both.

Increasing Visibility Fast

Quick-response marketing is all about getting noticed fast and bringing in a steady flow of new clients. It's especially useful when launching a practice, promoting a new service, or filling last-minute openings. These strategies often involve paid ads or local promotions, and while they can work fast, they do come at a cost, so it's important to spend wisely.

Too often, counsellors invest in ads before refining their messaging or optimising their website, leading to poor results. If your website doesn't clearly tell potential clients who you are, what you do, and why they should book with you, even the best ad campaign won't convert.

Most Effective Quick-Response Marketing Options

1. Meta (Facebook & Instagram) Ads: These ads work by grabbing attention in a scrolling feed, meaning they're engagement-based and speak ethically and directly to your ideal client's pain points. A generic ad like, 'Now taking new clients,' won't perform well. Something like, 'Struggling with anxiety but too exhausted to talk about it? Here's where to start,' will get much more engagement.

2. Google Ads: Unlike social media ads, Google Ads target keywords that people type into the search bar. If someone types, 'grief counselling near me,' they're already looking for a service, making them a much warmer lead. However, Google Ads are the vehicle to your website, so are only effective if your website is strong.

3. Local Advertising: Community bulletin boards, GP clinics, and local newspapers might seem old-school, but they still work—especially in regional areas. If you're building an in-person practice, visibility in your local community matters; building a presence within your community is important.

The challenge with quick-response marketing is that it only works while you're actively running ads or promotions. Once you stop, so do the enquiries. That's why you need long-term strategies that create a steady stream of referrals and organic traffic. My top tip here is to learn these ad strategies properly or hire someone reliable; otherwise, you're playing roulette with your money.

Long-Term Marketing: Creating a Consistent Client Flow

Long-term marketing strategies can feel like an effort as the results aren't about direct sales (like paid advertising). It's about setting up your practice and your brand for steady, ongoing growth. Rather than constantly paying for ads, these strategies help clients find you naturally, so you're not always pushing for visibility. It's about building your credibility, your brand and the 'know, like and trust factor'. Potential clients often need between 7-15 touchpoints (or contact) with you through your various marketing aspects, depending on how ready they are to engage counselling services.

One of the most powerful long-term strategies is building strong referral networks, as clients listen to people they already know regarding referrals. Yet, many counsellors neglect this because it takes time, effort and consistency and getting a tad uncomfortable at times (especially for us introverts!).

The Power of Referral Pathways

Referrals remain one of the most effective and ethical ways to grow a practice. When a trusted professional refers a client to you, that person arrives already confident in your skills and more likely to commit to therapy.

But referrals don't just happen—you have to build and maintain those connections, get comfortable with feeling uncomfortable and used to hearing the words, 'Not at this time'. Remember that most people don't know you, so a no isn't a personal rejection.

Here's what can work:

- Identify key referral resources: Use the market research you've already done to create a target list of potential referral partners. This could include GPs, allied health professionals, schools, funeral homes, community centres, support groups, and even alternative therapists. Think beyond the obvious; hairdressers, fitness coaches, and financial advisors all work with people facing life challenges and might be open to referring to you.

- Get in front of them in person: Cold emails rarely work. People are busy and delete them. If you want referrals, you need to show up. Drop into medical centres, introduce yourself to practice managers, attend networking events, or offer free lunch-and-learn talks for local businesses.

- Make it easy for people to refer to you: A referral is not just about trust, it's about convenience. If a physiotherapist has to search for your contact details, they'll refer to someone else instead. Have business cards, an easy-to-navigate website, and a simple way for people to connect with you.

- Keep the relationship alive: Too many counsellors introduce themselves once and never follow up. Stay on people's radar. Send occasional updates, share helpful resources, and check in periodically.

- Be a giver, not just a taker: If you want referrals, be willing to refer out too. If a client isn't the right fit for you, connecting them with someone who is builds goodwill. Over time, the professionals you refer to will return the favour.

Other Key Long-Term Marketing Strategies

While referrals are a major focus, other long-term strategies also play a role in keeping your practice visible and growing over time.

- Search Engine Optimisation (SEO) and blogging: A well-optimised website ensures that people find you organically when searching for your services. Blogging isn't about writing long essays, it's about answering the questions your ideal clients are already asking.

- Social media presence: You don't need to be on every platform, choose the one or two where your ideal clients hang out. If LinkedIn doesn't make sense for you, don't use it. If TikTok makes you cringe, skip it. The key is consistency.

- Community engagement: Free talks, guest speaking, and running local workshops help build credibility and visibility. If your community doesn't know you exist, how can they refer to you?

Bringing It All Together: A Balanced Marketing Plan

Marketing isn't about doing everything, it's about doing the right things at the right time.

- If you're brand new, focus on setting up your website, referral networks, and a simple social media presence. Don't waste money on ads if your foundations aren't in place.

- If you're struggling to get enquiries, revisit your messaging, does it clearly communicate who you help and why? If referrals are slow, are you following up and staying visible to referral partners?

- If your practice is steady but you want to grow, layer in SEO, blogging, and email marketing for long-term sustainability.

Marketing is about building a practice that attracts clients naturally, not chasing them. By combining quick-response strategies for visibility with long-term relationship-building and brand positioning, you'll create a steady and reliable flow of clients. Instead of stressing about income and scrambling for bookings, you'll have people coming to you because they already know, like, and trust you.

Section Seven: Your Website – Your Practice's Shopfront

In today's digital world, your website is your counselling practice's shopfront—it's where potential clients will form their first impression of you. It's no longer enough to rely solely on word of mouth or social media; people will Google you before they ever reach out. If you don't have a website, or if your site doesn't make sense, has a poor user experience or isn't optimised for mobile, you could be losing potential clients before they've even had the chance to connect with you. I personally don't engage a business that doesn't have a website. I move on to someone else.

Your website should work for you, not against you. A well-thought-out site enhances credibility, ensures your message reaches the right audience, and acts as a silent but powerful sales tool. But a bad website? That can actively hurt your business, making you seem unprofessional, outdated, or even untrustworthy.

Choosing the Right Platform

Choosing the right platform for your website is a very important decision. Don't skip this step because you just want the cheapest or easiest option—do your research! There are plenty of options out there like WordPress, Squarespace, Wix, GoDaddy, and others, but each comes with pros and cons. The key is to select a platform that balances ease of use with the level of control you need.

Some platforms, like Wix and Squarespace, are all-in-one solutions, offering simple drag-and-drop website builders with built-in hosting and security. They're great if you want something easy to set up and maintain, but they do come with limitations. You don't own your site in the same way you do with a platform like WordPress. WordPress, while more complex, gives you far more control, flexibility, and scalability. However, it does require maintenance and technical knowledge (or a developer who can assist when needed).

Before fully deciding, think about:

- Your technical ability: Are you comfortable with learning some tech or expanding your current knowledge? If not, outsourcing to someone to build is a good move but you need to know the basics; never hand your website over to someone due to tech terror!

- Your long-term needs: Will your website need custom features (courses, membership, etc.), an integrated booking system, or a blog?

- Your budget: Are you investing in a professionally built site, or will you be DIY-ing it? If you're outsourcing, get recommendations and do your research, as there are plenty of dodgy website developers out there.

Whatever platform you choose, remember that you must be able to access and update your website yourself. Being dependent on a developer for every small change will quickly become frustrating, expensive, and not viable long term.

What Makes a Website Work?

A website isn't just about looking good, it needs to function well and guide potential clients toward taking action. A high-converting website should be:

- User-friendly: Your website should be clean, easy to navigate, and mobile-responsive. Most people initially view websites on their phones and Google prioritises mobile optimisation, but we tend to build on a desktop and sometimes forget to fix the mobile version.

- SEO-optimised: If your site isn't appearing in Google searches, it's an invisible shop front. SEO (Search Engine Optimisation) helps your site get found, but it's not just about throwing in random keywords, it requires strategy. Writing blog posts, using the right search terms, and structuring your content correctly all impact your visibility. Getting help here might be necessary but proceed with caution and only use people who are recommended.

- Clear client-focused copywriting: Many counsellors make the mistake of treating their website like a CV or an academic paper! Clients generally don't worry too much about where you studied or what certifications you hold (at least not initially), they generally believe you're qualified and want to know whether you understand their struggles and can help. Your website copy should speak to your ideal client, using their language and addressing their pain points, not just listing your qualifications.

- Branded and professional: Your site should reflect your practice's brand—consistent colours, fonts, and imagery matter. Investing in branding photos can make a huge difference in how professional and credible you appear.

When a Website Hurts Your Marketing More Than It Helps

A poorly designed website isn't just ineffective, it actively damages your practice. If your site is cluttered, slow to load, hard to navigate, or looks outdated, potential clients won't stick around long enough to book an appointment. Think about how you feel when you land on a website that's dreadful. Worse, if the information is unclear or they can't easily contact you, they'll move on to someone else—quickly!

Many counsellors spend money on ads, social media, and other marketing efforts only to be frustrated that they're not getting bookings. More often than not, the problem isn't the marketing, it's that their website isn't converting visitors into clients. Before you even think about spending money on ads, you need to ensure your website is doing its job.

DIY vs. Hiring a Designer – Where to Invest

This is a common question, I've personally done a mix of both, I built my own current WordPress website and am very proud of what I achieved, but I also had some help and ongoing maintenance from my wonderful developer. There's no right or wrong answer but ponder these points:

- If you're tech-savvy and willing to learn, DIY can be cost-effective. However, it's time-consuming, and if done poorly, it'll end up costing you more to fix it.

- If you hire a professional, make sure they understand your industry. A general website designer may not know how to structure a counselling site effectively for client conversion. Make sure they're recommended.

- If you use WordPress, you'll need to factor in hosting, ongoing maintenance, security updates, backups, and plugin updates, which are essential. If you're not comfortable managing this, you may need to pay for ongoing support.

Ultimately, your website is an investment in your business, whether in time, money, or both. Do it right the first time, and it'll pay for itself in credibility, client bookings, and long-term success.

Important note: moving a website to another platform can be done but it can also impact your SEO and visibility for some time. Start how you want to finish!

Section Eight: Measuring Marketing Metrics

Investing time, energy and money in the marketing strategies we've discussed without checking what's working is like running sessions without ever asking your clients how they're going! Understanding your metrics helps you track your investment, make informed decisions, adjust what's not working, and focus on what actually brings in clients. Let's start with website analytics.

Google has two free tools that help you track the metrics on your website: Google Analytics and Google Search Console. These tools provide great insight into who's visiting your site, how they found you, and which pages they spend the most time on. Warning! These are not the easiest to set up and understand (especially if you're not a data nerd), so maybe get some help on this.

Client enquiries also provide valuable information. Are people finding you through referrals, your contact form, Psychology Today, or social media? Tracking these sources allows you to see where your efforts are paying off. If you're getting lots of enquiries but few bookings, there's a disconnect, whether it's unclear messaging, pricing concerns, or attracting the wrong audience. Keeping a simple spreadsheet of enquiries, sources, and conversion rates can highlight trends and areas to improve.

For those running email marketing campaigns, platforms like Mailchimp or Mailerlite offer data on open rates and engagement. If few people are opening your emails, it may be time to tweak subject lines or adjust your content strategy.

Paid advertising metrics are particularly important. Whether you're running Facebook, Google, or LinkedIn ads, reviewing conversion rates will tell you whether your money is being well spent and how much each click is costing. If ads are generating clicks but no bookings, your website or ad copy may need adjusting.

Beyond numbers, return on investment (ROI) isn't just about money, it's also about time and energy. If you're spending hours on social media with little engagement, is it worth it? If a referral network is consistently sending high-quality clients, nurture that relationship. The goal is to work smarter, not harder by focusing on what's actually bringing in results.

Tracking doesn't have to be complicated, but it does need to be consistent. Keeping a pulse on your marketing efforts means you're making informed decisions, otherwise you might as well flush your money down the toilet!

Ethical Sales and Client Retention

Ethical sales and client retention in private practice go beyond professionalism—they're about our ethical code's integrity, respecting client autonomy, and always putting client care ahead of your business goals and income needs. Counsellors aren't regulated under AHPRA, which means we don't have the same strict advertising guidelines as psychologists, but that doesn't mean we can operate without ethical considerations.

One common concern I see, particularly among some new counsellors, is an eagerness to secure clients that can sometimes cross into what I would call chasing clients. This might look like excessive follow-ups after an initial inquiry or multiple emails encouraging a past client to return. While follow-ups are important, there's a fine line between offering support and making clients feel pressured. If someone doesn't book in after an initial enquiry, or they decide not to return after a few sessions, that decision must be respected. A single follow-up is appropriate, but anything beyond that can feel like a sales push rather than client care. I understand the struggle here, it's tricky to know how far is too far sometimes, but the question to answer is, 'What is the motivation behind calling the client again?'

Another issue that can arise is the hesitancy to refer a client elsewhere, even when it's clear they would be better seen by someone else. This often stems from financial worry. I understand this fear, but holding onto a client who needs a different kind of support is not just unethical, it can also be damaging to the client and to your reputation as a professional. Trust is built when we act in the best interests of our clients, even if that means referring them to someone better suited to their needs.

Financial stress can also lead some counsellors to continue working when they're personally or professionally unwell. Whether it's illness, injury, personal stress, or burnout, there are times when stepping back is necessary. Clients can tell when we're emotionally or mentally drained and pushing through out of financial necessity isn't an ethical way to run a business, nor can it be sustained for long periods.

If you're in a position where missing a week of work would leave you in financial distress, it may be time to consider supplementary income while your practice grows. Contracting, part-time work, or even a non-counselling-related job can help relieve the pressure, allowing you to operate from a place of confidence rather than desperation.

At its core, ethical sales and client retention are about ensuring every interaction, from marketing to long-term client relationships, is built on respect, professionalism, and integrity. Private practice is a journey, not a destination, and maintaining ethical standards is what allows you to build a solid reputation, attract the right clients, and create a practice that's both financially viable and true to your values.

Let's chat about those doubts!

I see you—the hesitation, the frustration, the quiet (or loud) voice of doubt asking, 'Far out! How am I going to do all this?'

Marketing can feel overwhelming, especially when it's outside your comfort zone, we all experience this, whether it's cold calling for referrals or being visible on social media. You may be doubting your ability to run a business. You're not alone. Every counsellor (including me) has faced that fear—the fear of getting it wrong, of wasting time, of feeling like an imposter in a space filled with others who seem to have it all figured out.

Maybe the idea of 'selling yourself' makes you cringe, or you're convinced that marketing is for extroverts, tech-savvy people, or those with big budgets. Maybe you've tried before and you're reading this book now because you're hoping it contains the secret sauce! You've put yourself out there, done all the things and had zero calls or emails. When that happens, it's easy to start second-guessing everything, seeing the dream rapidly fading.

But here's what I want you to know: first, you're not alone in this, everyone has experienced this at some point (if they say they don't I suspect they're telling stories). Marketing isn't about being pushy, flashy, or someone you're not. It's about forming a genuine connection. It's about showing up in a way that feels true to you, so the people who need your services can find you. You don't need to do it all.

Marketing Backrest – Support for Business Growth

You don't need to be perfect. You just need to start taking small, intentional steps forward.

We tell our clients they're unique! Well, *you* are unique—you have something valuable to offer that no one else does because you're not them. And your future clients? They're out there, searching for exactly what you bring. The more you step forward, the easier it gets. One action at a time, one connection at a time, one client at a time.

How's Counsellor Casey Going?

Casey stares at their screen, fingers hovering over the mouse. Their website editor is open—again. They've rewritten their about page three times this week, but something still feels off. It doesn't sound like them. It sounds professional, sure, but kind of boring and bland!

They groan, closing the tab. Marketing is exhausting, they didn't realise it would be like this. They know it's important. They know they need to get their name out there. But between the endless tweaks to their website, second-guessing social media posts, and the awkwardness of talking about themselves, it feels like a full-time job on top of actually seeing clients.

And speaking of clients…where are they all?

They glance at their email inbox, hoping for an enquiry. Nothing. A small pang of self-doubt creeps in. *What if I'm doing all of this for nothing?*

Determined not to spiral, Casey pulls up the list of website edits they've been avoiding. Their supervisor had suggested making the site more personal, less formal, and more inviting. People needed to feel like I was talking to them as soon as they landed on the page.

So, they get to work. They add a photo of themselves—not a stiff, posed headshot, but one where they actually look like the kind of counsellor they'd want to see. They tweak the wording in their services section to speak directly to their ideal client instead of just listing credentials. They even—after much hesitation—record a short welcome video for the homepage. It feels cringeworthy at first, but once they watch it back, it's…not bad actually.

Then, something clicks. They've been trying to be everything to everyone. Their website, their messaging, and even their posts on social media were broad and generic, designed to appeal to 'anyone who needed support'. But that wasn't the kind of practice Casey had dreamed of building.

With that realisation, they go back to the drawing board. Who do they actually want to work with? Who are the clients that light them up?

After reflecting on past experiences, Casey realises they're most engaged when supporting people going through major life transitions—career changes, relationship shifts, adjusting to parenthood. That's where they feel the most impact.

Armed with this clarity, they start digging into what other counsellors in their area are doing. A quick search reveals that the market is flooded with generalist counsellors, but no one is speaking directly to the challenges of life transitions. There's a space for Casey to nicely position themselves. Casey's confidence increases just a little.

Making changes to their website no longer feels like aimless tinkering coming from doubt. The words become more specific and intentional. Instead of vague statements about supporting 'anyone who needs help,' they now speak directly to people feeling stuck, overwhelmed, or uncertain about their next step in life.

Marketing Backrest – Support for Business Growth

It feels uncomfortable at first, what if they're limiting themselves too much? What if people think I don't see anyone else and leave? But the moment they hit publish, something shifts. The next few enquiries are different. People are booking because they resonate with Casey's message, not just because they're the first available counsellor.

Next on the list is referral pathways!

This part is stretching Casey right out of their comfort zone. When employed Casey could do this in their sleep but this is different. The thought of walking into another professional's space and saying, 'Hey, refer clients to me!' makes them want to crawl under a rock.

But logically, they know it's not about selling themselves. It's about building relationships.

So, they start small. They send a friendly email to a local physio they used to work with, just letting them know they've started their practice and are available if any of their clients need mental health support. No pressure, no expectation, just a simple, 'Here's what I do if you ever need someone to refer to.'

To their surprise, the physio replies within the hour. 'Great to hear! Let's catch up soon.'

Casey exhales. That wasn't too hard, it was effort, but doable.

Later that week, a new client enquiry lands in their inbox. It's a referral from a dietitian they'd briefly connected with on social media. A small win, but a real one.

Sitting back, Casey realises something important. Marketing isn't about doing everything perfectly, it's about showing up, step by step.

For the first time, instead of feeling overwhelmed, they felt that they had made some progress, and the doubtful chatter was lessening.

Action Steps

1. Identifying Your Ideal Clients

Write a detailed client avatar including demographics, values, challenges, and goals. Describe the kind of clients you want more of—and why.

2. Market Research and Finding Your Place in the Industry

Create a spreadsheet to track competitor pricing, services, referral sources, and gaps in the market. Identify at least one gap you could fill.

3. Niching vs. Specialisation: Positioning Yourself Correctly

Choose one to three niche areas based on your skills, interests, and market demand. Refine your focus without boxing yourself in.

4. Creating Your Unique Selling Proposition (USP)

Craft a one-sentence USP using this formula:

'I help [target client] with [problem] so they can [outcome]'. Refine until it's clear and compelling.

5. Building Your Brand Identity

Write a brand story in a few sentences—why you became a counsellor, what you stand for, and how you help. Ensure your visual branding (colours, logo, fonts) aligns with it.

6. Marketing Strategies: Quick vs. Long-Term Approaches

Select one quick-response strategy (e.g., Google Ads, social media ads) and one long-term strategy (e.g., blogging, SEO, networking). Implement both.

7. Websites and Online Presence

Research which platform you will use for your website. Or if you already have a website, conduct an evaluation and check for these essentials: clear messaging, mobile-friendly design, strong call-to-action, SEO basics, and up-to-date branding.

8. Measuring Marketing Metrics

Set up Google Analytics & Search Console (if not already done) and start tracking where your last five clients came from. Adjust based on what's working.

9. Ethical Sales and Client Retention

Review your client follow-up process. Ensure its professional and ethical—no excessive chasing, just clear, supportive communication

'Your talent determines what you can do. Your motivation determines how much you are willing to do. Your attitude determines how well you will do it.'

— Lou Holtz

Chapter 7

STRONG ARMRESTS: CONFIDENT CLINICAL PROCESSES

*'Wisdom is not a product of schooling but of
the lifelong attempt to acquire it.'*
Albert Einstein

You can have the best branding, the shiniest booking system, and a rock-solid marketing plan, but if your clinical work isn't strong, ethical, and effective, none of it matters. Clients won't stay, referrals won't come, and your practice will struggle to grow. Your practice and reputation rest on your skills as a counsellor—you're the service of the business.

The Counsellors Chair

Resting on a Solid Private Practice

The armrests of the chair represent the clinical practice of a counsellor—the solid support structure that our practice rests on. This chapter isn't about learning how to be a counsellor. This chapter is about ensuring that your skills, ethics, and professional commitments are at the level they need to be for continued business growth and an effective, ethical private practice.

Being a counsellor isn't just about being good with people. It's about competence, accountability, and professional integrity. The moment you let any of this slip, your practice will struggle, not just in reputation but in real client outcomes. If the skills the counsellor is leaning on aren't well developed, it leads to unstable sessions, unmet expectations, and ultimately, clients disengaging from therapy altogether.

Why Solid Clinical Foundations Matter

Counsellors who are confident in their skills feel different, to themselves, to their clients, and to their professional peers. When you trust your own competence, you stop second-guessing every session. You no longer walk out of appointments wondering, Did I say the right thing? Did I miss something? Am I actually helping? Instead, you know you're providing ethical, effective support. This isn't arrogance or cockiness! It's about having the right foundations in place so that you can work with presence and professionalism.

Beyond the counselling room, professional credibility and ethical integrity go hand in hand. The most respected counsellors in our industry aren't those who simply meet professional standards but those who strive for excellence. Remaining sharp through ongoing learning, engaging in supervision, and being reflective about your practice ensures that your work continues to evolve with the field.

When these foundations are in place, your practice doesn't just function, it flourishes. You're not constantly scrambling to feel competent, fix mistakes, or chase down referrals that aren't coming. Instead, your confidence and skills create a ripple effect—clients trust you, word-of-mouth referrals increase, and your reputation grows. A thriving practice isn't about luck; it's about strong, ethical, and well-supported clinical processes.

Wobbly Clinical Practices?

It doesn't take long for cracks to show without these processes. Doubt can creep in. You might find yourself second-guessing interventions, unsure of how to handle complex client situations, or feeling overwhelmed when a session doesn't go as planned.

Clients pick up on this uncertainty. They may not be able to articulate exactly what feels off, but they sense when a counsellor lacks confidence or direction. This can make them hesitant to open up, less engaged in the therapeutic process, or even unsure whether they want to continue. And if trust erodes, it can be difficult, sometimes impossible, to rebuild.

A lack of clear clinical processes can also take a toll on you. The emotional intensity of counselling is already high, but without strong boundaries, supervision, and skill development, it can feel like you're constantly running on empty. Over time, the accumulation of stress, uncertainty, and self-doubt can leave you questioning whether private practice is for you.

The goal isn't perfection—it's professional growth and accountability. No counsellor has all the answers, and we're always learning, but those with well-established clinical foundations know where to seek support, how to reflect on their work, and when to refine their skills. This is what allows a practice to feel stable, fulfilling, and built for the long haul.

In this chapter, we're exploring the clinical side of private practice: the skills, ethics, and professional commitments that ensure we actually are providing quality, ethical support to our clients. These are the armrests of our work; the things we lean on every single day to do this job well. We'll cover the critical components of strong clinical practice. Supervision is the vital pillar of support, reflection and guidance. Strong boundaries that create sustainability, ensuring both you and your clients are protected in the therapeutic space. Ongoing professional development keeps your skills relevant and your practice fresh and effective.

While this chapter won't cover how to be a counsellor, it will focus on the professional and ethical responsibilities that should already be in place. This book assumes that you are either a qualified counsellor or on your way to being one through appropriate study. If you're looking for an in-depth clinical guide, that's outside the scope of this book.

Supervision – Your Professional Safety Net

You'll notice this is a topic I keep coming back to and that's deliberate because it's that important. Supervision isn't just a nice-to-have or a 'when I feel like it or can afford it'—it's the backbone of ethical practice. It's what keeps us accountable, sharp, and professionally responsible. Yet, every now and then, I come across a counsellor who believes they can go it alone or doesn't want to invest in regular

Strong Armrests: Confident Clinical Processes

supervision. They may not have the self-awareness established yet to realise how in need of supervision they really are. Let me be clear: there's no place for lone rangers in this profession.

Working in private practice without supervision is like a surgeon skipping sterile procedures. Risky, unprotected, and absolutely not set up for success or client care.

Supervision isn't about ticking a box or just meeting your association's requirements. It's a lifeline, a space where you can unpack difficult cases, challenge your own biases, and reflect on your work without fear of judgement.

It's also where you get the support you need. No matter how long you've been in this profession, there will always be cases that sit with you long after the session ends. Clients whose stories bring up unexpected emotions. Situations that leave you second-guessing yourself. Ethical grey areas that feel impossible to navigate alone.

Supervision gives you a structured, professional space to reflect on those moments. To talk through client challenges in a way that's both constructive and growth-oriented. It's where you can acknowledge and explore your own triggers—those moments where a client's words, actions, or situation unexpectedly press on something personal within you.

And we all have them.

No one enters this profession as a blank slate. We bring our own experiences, worldviews, and personal histories into the room, whether we realise it or not. And if we're not aware of how those things influence our work, they can show up in ways that aren't always helpful to the client.

A good supervision relationship helps you examine your assumptions, unpack your biases, and challenge unconscious patterns that may be influencing the way you approach client work. Without it, you risk becoming reactive rather than reflective, making decisions based on personal perspective rather than professional best practice.

Without supervision, you leave yourself vulnerable. Not just to burnout or emotional fatigue, but to errors in judgement—the kind that happen when we're exhausted, overwhelmed, or too deep in our own work to see things objectively.

It's also where you are held accountable. Because no matter how experienced or knowledgeable we are, we all have blind spots. We all have cases that shake us. We all have moments where we doubt ourselves or feel out of our depth. A strong supervision relationship means you're never truly alone in this work.

I can't count the number of times supervision has helped me navigate complex cases, ethical dilemmas, or those moments where the emotional weight of the job felt just a little too heavy. Having a supervisor who understands your work, challenges you when necessary, and provides a safe space to process the hard stuff is invaluable.

It doesn't matter whether you've been in practice for one year or 40 years, we all need supervision. We all need accountability. And in private practice, where you don't have colleagues next to you every day, it becomes even more essential.

Building Competence and Adaptability in Client Work

One of the biggest transitions from training to practice is realising that counselling isn't just about what you know, it's about how you apply it. Private practice, in particular, demands a level of adaptability that no textbook can fully prepare you for. There's a stark difference between sitting in a classroom discussing theories and sitting across from a client who's relying on you for real, tangible support.

For many new counsellors, the first few months or couple of years of private practice can feel overwhelming. Suddenly, you're responsible for more than just your clinical work. You're making decisions about who you see, how you work, carrying the risk and when to refer. Without the structure of an organisation or a team of colleagues to bounce ideas off, the weight of responsibility settles in quickly.

But here's the thing, no counsellor starts out feeling completely confident. Confidence is built through experience, supervision, and ongoing professional development. It grows as you lean into the work, refine how we work as we go and know where to further develop. The key is to embrace the process of growth while ensuring that you're providing ethical, competent care from the very start.

Bridging the Gap Between Theory and Practice

When I first moved into private practice, I already had years of experience working in schools, supporting young people and their families. I knew I was competent; I had built strong clinical skills through hands-on experience. But stepping into private practice was a whole different ballgame. Suddenly, I didn't have a well-being team down the hall to debrief with. I didn't have a line manager to consult when an ethical dilemma arose. It was just me, my clients, and the reality of being fully responsible for every clinical decision I made.

That shift can knock your confidence, no matter how skilled you are. It's one thing to know your modalities and interventions, it's another to realise that you're on your own!

For those transitioning straight from study to private practice, this gap can feel even wider. Working in an organisation allows you to gain valuable experience and sometimes gain supervision to assist you along the way. Private practice requires you to step into the work without that built-in organisational support. That's why, as counsellors in private practice, we need to be clear about the reason we're going into business to start with—what's our motivation? We must always reflect on our existing skills, understand our competence, identify areas for growth, and take action.

If you're moving from an agency or organisational setting, take the time to assess what clinical skills you've already developed and how they transfer to the private practice space. If you're starting fresh without prior experience, be intentional about building a solid foundation, through supervision, professional development, and leaning into communities of other counsellors who can provide guidance and encouragement.

One of the biggest realisations I had early in my career was that no single modality is perfect. Every therapeutic approach has its strengths and limitations, and no two clients are the same. That's why I take an integrative approach to counselling, I draw from multiple modalities and interventions to suit the client's needs, rather than sticking rigidly to one framework.

That said, there are counsellors who prefer a purist approach, working exclusively within one model, whether that's Person-Centred Therapy, CBT, ACT, or another modality. There's no right or wrong approach, what matters is that you have a solid grasp of your chosen frameworks and apply them with confidence and competence.

Strong Armrests: Confident Clinical Processes

The key isn't just knowing theories but knowing how to use them effectively. It's about developing the clinical intuition to understand when a particular approach fits and when it doesn't. And that only comes with time, practice, and a commitment to continuous learning.

The Reality of Private Practice: Facing the Gaps

No matter how comprehensive your training is, there will always be gaps when you transition from study to practice. And that's okay. Your qualification is your starting point, not the destination; we're life-long learners.

As someone who spent seven years training counsellors in diploma, advanced diploma, and graduate diploma courses, I can tell you with certainty that no course can fully prepare you for everything you'll encounter in practice. Counselling is an evolving field. Clients are complex. The human condition is complex. Situations arise that aren't covered in textbooks.

And yet, I see many new counsellors hesitate to fully step into their role because they feel they 'aren't ready'. The truth is, you'll never feel completely ready. Competence doesn't come from waiting, it comes from doing the work within your scope, under quality supervision.

The biggest challenge many new private practitioners face isn't necessarily a lack of skill—it's the sheer volume of information, complexity, and nuance that clients bring into the room. It's one thing to understand theories and interventions in training, but in practice, issues don't present in neat, textbook-style categories. Clients arrive in our counselling room and share with us their pain, stories, feelings, secrets and life experiences. At times, this can feel messy and overwhelming to a counsellor and before you know it, you're wondering:

- Where do I even start?
- What's the best approach in this situation?
- Am I covering everything that matters—have I missed something?

We've all been there, those wobbly moments. But it isn't about having all the answers, it's about empathy, understanding and compassion, it's about learning to navigate complexity whilst remaining within your scope of practice. That's why effective supervision, ongoing professional development, and connecting with peers isn't just helpful, it's essential. When you have support in making sense of client work, you can stop feeling paralysed by 'what do I do now?' and instead trust in your ability to unpack, assess, and move forward with confidence.

Preparing for the Unexpected

Even the most seasoned counsellors face situations where they feel out of their depth. Every client is different, and there will always be moments when you feel like you're floundering. The key isn't to have all the answers, it's to have the self-awareness and professional integrity to recognise your limits, seek support, and know when to refer.

One of the hardest lessons to learn in private practice is that you can't be everything to every client. Some clients won't be the right fit for you, some will present with issues outside your expertise, and some will need more than what you can ethically provide.

Knowing when to pause, consult, and refer isn't a failure, it's a sign of professional maturity. It's what separates ethical counsellors from those who overextend themselves, risking harm to both clients and themselves.

Private practice is a different path for everyone. Whether you're fresh out of your qualification, moving from an organisational setting, or are years into the profession, you bring unique skills, strengths, and areas for growth. Clinical work isn't about knowing everything, because you never will! It's about committing to lifelong learning and ethical practice, and surrounding yourself with the right support.

Boundaries – The Vital Key to Ethical and Effective Counselling

Boundaries in private practice aren't just professional guidelines; they're the invisible boundary line that ensures your work remains ethical, viable for the long term, and has the highest degree of client care. Without boundaries, counsellors risk blurred relationships, emotional exhaustion, and ethical errors that can compromise both their clients' well-being and their own professional integrity.

Every counsellor will have slightly different views on boundaries, informed by their ethical codes of practice, and shaped by their training, theoretical background, and personal experiences. But at the core, boundaries serve a simple yet crucial purpose: they create a safe and contained space for therapy, where both counsellor and client know what to expect. Without them, therapy can feel unpredictable, inconsistent, and at times, even unsafe.

Boundaries in Private Practice

When I first started in private practice, I already had strong professional boundaries from my experience working in schools. But even so, I quickly realised how different it felt to hold those boundaries when I was the only person responsible for enforcing them. In organisational settings, there were clear structures in place, including policies, admin staff handling parent inquiries, a team of well-being staff to bounce things off and a dependable line manager. But in private practice, suddenly, I was the one making every decision and carrying all the risk.

Many counsellors transitioning into private practice struggle with this shift. When no one else is enforcing the rules, it's easy to start shifting them. But small boundary breaches quickly become patterns, and once a pattern is set, it's much harder to correct.

At first, a counsellor might not even realise their boundaries are slipping. Maybe they start responding to client emails late at night, or they let sessions run over time. Perhaps they allow payment delays because it feels uncomfortable to chase up money. But these seemingly small actions start to erode the framework that holds the therapeutic process together.

Without clear boundaries, sessions start to feel more chaotic, professional roles blur into your personal life and counsellors may find themselves thinking about clients long after hours. Over time, these small boundary issues can lead to burnout, resentment, and even ethical or legal consequences.

The Fine Line Between Professional and Personal Boundaries

Personal and professional boundaries are connected—we can't separate our personal self from our work self. If a counsellor struggles with boundaries in their personal life, if they have difficulty saying no, feel responsible for others' emotions, give in to expectations, or tend to overextend themselves, it will almost certainly show up in their client work.

This is where self-awareness is critical. If you find yourself frequently feeling stretched thin, struggling to enforce limits, or feeling a strong emotional pull to 'fix' a client's problems, it's worth reflecting on where that comes from. These patterns are often shaped by deeper beliefs about responsibility, worth, and the fear of disappointing others.

This isn't a flaw, it's human. But recognising these tendencies and working on them, whether through supervision or personal therapy, is essential for any counsellor who wants to maintain professionalism while also protecting their own well-being.

Modelling Healthy Boundaries for Clients

One of the most important, and often overlooked, aspects of boundary-setting in private practice is that we're modelling healthy boundaries for our clients. Many people seek counselling because they struggle with boundaries in their personal lives, whether that's feeling constantly taken advantage of, being unable to say no, or carrying the weight of other people's expectations.

If we, as counsellors, fail to model good boundaries, we reinforce the very patterns that clients are trying to change.

Clients are constantly learning from our professional conduct, often in ways they don't consciously recognise. Simple actions, like holding firm to session times, maintaining professional distance, and communicating clearly, send a message about what healthy boundaries look like in practice.

For example, if a client repeatedly arrives late, we hold to the scheduled session time rather than extending it. If a client pushes for extra contact between sessions, we gently but clearly reinforce the purpose and limits of therapy. If a client tries to overstep professional boundaries by asking overly personal questions, we redirect the conversation rather than engage.

These small but consistent actions teach clients what it means to hold and respect boundaries, often in ways they may not have experienced before.

When Clients Push Boundaries

There will always be clients who test or challenge boundaries. Some may request personal details about your life, contact you outside of agreed hours, or consistently miss payments. Others may overshare in emails, writing lengthy messages between sessions that subtly shift the dynamic from structured therapy to an open-ended emotional outlet.

It may be tempting to move our boundaries, maybe it feels like an act of kindness, or maybe it's just easier to avoid the discomfort of enforcing a boundary. But small boundary breaches quickly become patterns, and once a pattern is set, it's much harder to correct.

This is where professional confidence comes in. Holding boundaries isn't about being harsh or rigid, it's about maintaining the structure that allows therapy to be effective. When boundaries are communicated clearly and compassionately, clients don't feel rejected or dismissed. Instead, they feel secure, knowing exactly what to expect from the therapeutic process.

Holding Boundaries Professionally

For many counsellors, the hardest part of boundaries isn't knowing what they should be, it's communicating them in a way that feels natural and professional.

In organisational settings, admin staff typically handle things like scheduling, payments, and policies. But in private practice, those responsibilities fall directly on the counsellor. Many new private practitioners find this aspect of the work challenging, not because they don't understand boundaries, but because enforcing them can feel uncomfortable at first.

The discomfort often comes from an icky feeling of dealing with these 'business' related matters in session and a fear of damaging the therapeutic relationship, but in reality, clients respect and respond well to clear, professionally communicated boundaries. They may not always like them in the moment, but they will trust you more for holding them consistently.

If you struggle to enforce boundaries, working with a supervisor to develop scripts or responses can help you feel more confident. Even practising how you'll phrase boundary-setting conversations can make them feel more natural when they arise in real time.

At the end of the day, boundaries aren't barriers, they're safety for all, they're the framework that allows you to provide ethical, competent counselling without resulting in harm to us or the client. If you want longevity in private practice, learning how to set, hold, and communicate your boundaries isn't just important, it's essential.

The Danger of Winging It – Neglecting Professional Development

Professional development is a topic we've already touched on in this book, particularly in relation to ethical obligations and business growth. But in this section, we're going to focus purely on its role in clinical competence, because when it comes to client care, ongoing learning isn't a luxury; it's a necessity.

In Australia, counselling remains a self-regulated profession. That means if you're a member of one of the peak associations, you're required to engage in a certain amount of OPD (ongoing professional development) each year to maintain membership. These built-in requirements are designed to ensure that as practitioners, we continue learning and refining our skills, rather than assuming our initial qualification is enough to sustain us for the next 30 years.

But here's the current industry reality, there's no external governing body ensuring counsellors stay competent. If you choose not to register with an association, there's no official requirement to engage in ongoing learning. That freedom comes with risk: without intentional development, it's easy to slip into stagnation, relying on the same knowledge and skill set year after year.

Counselling is an evolving field. Research, theories, and interventions are constantly shifting. Clients are presenting with increasingly complex issues, and our role is to keep up, not coast. Private practice is particularly risky in this regard because there's no workplace mandating additional training. The responsibility falls entirely on us to assess our gaps, challenge our assumptions, and actively pursue growth.

Competence vs. Complacency

Most counsellors I meet don't fall into the trap of arrogance, if anything, it's the opposite. Some struggle with imposter syndrome, questioning whether they're skilled enough, experienced enough, or qualified enough to be effective. The idea of being too confident in one's abilities is not as common in this profession.

But that doesn't mean complacency isn't a problem.

Some practitioners, particularly those with years of experience, may inadvertently develop complacency in their assumed knowledge. Thinking that because they've been in the field a long time, they already know all they need to know. The reality is that no matter how long you've been a counsellor, you'll encounter clients who bring issues beyond your current skill set. You'll be challenged. You'll sit in sessions where you realise your knowledge on a particular issue is outdated, incomplete, or simply not enough.

What you do in those moments determines the kind of practitioner you are.

Do you assume you can figure it out and proceed anyway? Or do you acknowledge your limitations and take active steps to fill the gaps, whether that's through further training, supervision, or referral?

For example, a counsellor who primarily works with individuals might start receiving inquiries about couples counselling. While they may have some general knowledge about relationship dynamics, couples therapy is an entirely different skill set. Without specific training, they could easily do more harm than good, reinforcing destructive patterns, failing to identify underlying dynamics, or even exacerbating conflict or harm.

The ethical response in this case isn't to wing it and hope for the best, it's to seek proper training, refer out when needed, and ensure they're genuinely competent before taking on the work.

That's the mindset every ethical practitioner needs to adopt.

The Ethical Responsibility to Keep Learning

There's a fine line between confidence and overconfidence. While it's important to trust your skills, it's equally important to recognise when a client presents with an issue beyond your scope of competence.

It's also important to remember that staying within your scope doesn't just mean avoiding areas you haven't been trained in, it also means keeping your existing skills sharp and relevant. Counselling isn't a static profession; best practices evolve, new interventions emerge, and research reshapes the way we understand mental health.

If we fail to keep learning, we risk working in outdated ways that may no longer serve clients as effectively as they once did. Our ethical guidelines make it clear: we must not mislead clients about our expertise. We cannot assume that because we're qualified counsellors, we're automatically competent in every area of counselling. That's why ongoing learning is not just beneficial, it's an ethical responsibility.

Strong Armrests: Confident Clinical Processes

Professional Isolation

A sad reality in private practice is professional isolation. Unlike working in an organisation, where team meetings, training programs, lunchtime chats and structured learning are built into the workplace culture, private practice means you're solely responsible for your own development and ongoing self-care.

There are multiple ways to be informed and feel connected and supported in what can be a lonely profession, such as:

- Group supervision: Engaging within a group that encourages collegial support can be a valuable mechanism to reduce isolation. I run several groups per month, and this is the number one thing that counsellors gain from the experience—knowing they're not alone.

- Peer discussions: Connect with other counsellors to exchange ideas, discuss client work (ethically and confidentially), and learn from shared experiences.

- Joining a community of counsellors: Online communities can be a great source of support if they're run well. Choose wisely. Counsellors Community Australia Facebook Group is one of the largest groups for Aussie Counsellors. We also have a premium Circle community for those who want that added support and connection (see details in the Next Steps chapter).

- Industry events: Go to association events like chapter meetings, networking events or conferences to meet other counsellors.

Ongoing learning and industry connection isn't just about keeping up with industry standards, it's about ensuring that every client who walks into your practice receives the best possible care. Because at the end of the day, professional growth isn't just about you—it's about them.

The Trap of Excessive Professional Development and Not Enough Practice

Learning is essential, but practical application matters more than just collecting certificates.

If complacency is one side of the spectrum, the other extreme is when professional development becomes a way to avoid stepping fully into practice. This is something I see often, particularly with newer counsellors, those who have recently graduated or those who carry a deep-seated belief that they're not good enough yet. If that's you, this is something to take to supervision, because the issue isn't a lack of skill, it's a story you're telling yourself.

It's easy to feel like there are endless gaps to fill. You graduate, relieved to finally be done with assignments, only to be hit with the realisation that now, the responsibility of client care rests entirely on you. Suddenly, the safety net of structured learning is gone, and instead of feeling ready, you feel unprepared.

So, you do what feels logical, you start filling those gaps as quickly as possible. You buy every book you can find, telling yourself you'll read them all (even though they end up collecting dust on your shelf). You sign up for every training that sounds remotely useful, stacking up courses faster than you can complete them. Maybe you even decide to go straight into another qualification—a Master's, PhD, or another diploma, convincing yourself that if you just get one more certification, you'll finally feel ready.

For some counsellors, this pattern serves a purpose. There are those who genuinely want to work in academia—to lecture, train, or contribute to research—and for them, pursuing multiple qualifications makes sense. But for others, professional development becomes a distraction rather than a tool for growth. Some counsellors become what I call professional students—moving from one qualification to another, staying in a cycle of learning because it feels safer than actually stepping into the work. The academic world is structured, predictable, and offers a sense of control. Private practice? That's the unknown. It's messy, it's real, and it comes with the discomfort of not always having the perfect answer.

While professional development is vital, when it becomes an avoidance strategy, it stops being about growth and starts being about hiding. Being so busy you have no time to practice the art of counselling.

But here's the truth: no amount of qualifications will ever make you feel fully 'ready'. There will always be more to learn.

You are exactly where you need to be right now.

If you're reading this and see yourself, if you recognise that you've been stacking up PD courses without actually applying the knowledge, then it's time to take a step back. Go read the Mindset chapter again. Revisit the section on comparison and running your own race. There's no ultimate destination where you suddenly feel like you've 'arrived' as a counsellor. Growth is continuous, and you don't need another $10,000 certification to prove your worth.

I say this from experience, not from a place of judgment. While I've never been someone drawn to academic study for the sake of it, I've fallen into the trap of collecting professional development. I've bought courses I never completed. I've stacked up training programs that sat untouched. I've invested in learning without taking the time to implement what I already knew. So, this isn't me preaching at you, it's me speaking as someone who has been there, done that and got the tee-shirt!

That's why I want to emphasise this: you don't need to know everything to start working effectively with clients. No one does.

The Power of Practising What You Know

At some point, you have to stop preparing and start doing.

No one masters a skill by studying alone. Every experienced counsellor you admire started exactly where you are, uncertain, figuring things out, making mistakes, learning from them, and growing. That's how mastery happens.

I still remember a lecturer who spoke at my graduation. She was someone I deeply respected, someone with decades of experience. And yet, she stood up in front of us and admitted that in her first few counselling sessions, she had no idea what she was doing.

She said, 'I asked them 'How do you feel about that?' And when I panicked and didn't know what to say next, I asked, 'What do you think you could do about that?' Those two questions got me through my first few sessions.'

And you know what? It worked. It was refreshing and reassuring to hear her say that.

Because clients don't need you to be perfect. They don't need you to have all the answers. They need you to show up, be present, listen, and offer a safe space for their counselling.

How you see experienced counsellors now is not how they started. The difference between them and you? They allowed themselves to be beginners and they're further down the road of their counselling journey.

So, if you're holding yourself back because you think you need just one more qualification before you're ready—stop. You're exactly where you need to be right now.

Go see clients. Do the work. Trust that you'll grow through experience.

Because you can't think your way into confidence. You have to step into it.

How's Counsellor Casey Doing?

Casey had expected private practice to feel like a natural next step. After all, they had worked their proverbial backside off getting their qualification. They had the passion and the drive. But once they were sitting in the counselling chair alone, with no manager down the hall and no team to consult, or the safety of placement, they thought, *I didn't realise how lonely private practice would be—it's quite scary when you realise that everything rests on you!*

They had spent years studying, but nothing quite prepared them for the moment a client sat across from them, waiting for support that suddenly felt weightier than it had in any role before. Theoretical knowledge didn't always translate neatly into real-life sessions. What if they missed something important or made a mistake?

At first, supervision felt like an obligation, an expense on a growing list, 'I was a bit resentful of supervision at first, to be honest. I hadn't enjoyed supervision in my placement, but this is different and helps me feel more confident and secure in what I am doing.'

Supervision had become a place to explore the self-doubt, a place to learn to trust their instincts instead of second-guessing every session. Casey now felt like a professional.

Professional development, on the other hand, became a rabbit hole. When Casey questioned their skills (which was frequently), they signed up for another training. More courses, more certificates, each one promising to fill the gaps. But instead of feeling more assured, they just felt increasingly overwhelmed, nothing was cementing itself. Eventually, they realised the problem wasn't a lack of knowledge, it was a lack of applying what they already knew. Learning was vital, but strategic learning—the kind that directly impacted their client work—was what needed to happen.

And then there were those pesky boundaries. The late-night emails, the sessions that ran over, and the guilt about applying their cancellation policy. Casey wanted to be helpful, available, and accommodating but they realised something critical, boundaries weren't just about protecting themselves, they were about protecting the integrity of the counselling space.

Strong Armrests: Confident Clinical Processes

Casey reflected, *clients don't need me to jump through rings of fire for them, they need someone who models good boundaries and limits.*

Casey still has moments of doubt and overwhelm—because who doesn't? But those moments no longer spiral into feeling frozen. 'I know there's no magic wand or secret handbook that I have missed out on. I know that feeling uncertain is normal and I'm learning how to manage it, and who to go to for support.'

Action Steps

1. Make Supervision Work for You

Before your next session, identify a clinical challenge, ethical dilemma, or boundary concern you'd like to unpack. Come prepared with questions and reflections so your supervision sessions actively support your growth, rather than just being a passive requirement.

2. Review Your Professional Development Budget and Plan

OPD can be expensive, and not all training is created equal. Go through your current or planned professional development spending and ask:

- Is this training directly relevant to the clients I see?

- Will this enhance my clinical skills in a meaningful way?

- Am I enrolling in this because I need it, or because I feel I 'should'?

Be intentional—prioritise learning that deepens your expertise rather than chasing qualifications for the sake of them.

3. Set a New Boundary and Practise Enforcing It

Boundaries are easy to understand in theory but harder to hold in practice. Identify one area where your boundaries with clients could be clearer, this might be communication outside of sessions, session times, or payment expectations. Write a clear, professional way to communicate this boundary and practise delivering it so you feel confident if a client pushes back.

4. Audit Your Scope and Referral Process

Take 10 minutes to write down the types of clients and issues you feel fully competent working with, and where your limits are. Now, create or update a referral list, and have a go-to plan for clients who need specialist support outside your expertise. If a complex case came in tomorrow, would you know exactly where to refer them? If not, this is the time to fix that.

5. Reflect on a Recent Ethical Dilemma or Decision

Think back to a moment in practice where you felt uncertain, maybe about a boundary, a disclosure, or a tricky client interaction. If you faced the same scenario again, how would you handle it differently? If you're unsure, bring it to supervision or discuss it with a peer. Ethical competence is built through reflection and dialogue, not just reading policies.

Strong Armrests: Confident Clinical Processes

'Decision is the spark that ignites action. Until a decision is made, nothing happens... Decision is the courageous facing of issues, knowing that if they are not faced, problems will remain forever unanswered.'
Wilferd A. Peterson

Chapter 8

PROTECTIVE WINGS – SELF-CARE THAT PREVENTS AND RESTORES

'Clients bring us their nightmares, drop them in our laps, and then leave us to sort them out for ourselves.'
Jeffrey Kottler

Do your eyes roll when you hear the words, 'You can't pour from an empty cup'? Heard it all before, right? But let's be honest, how often do we actually listen? Do we practice what we preach to clients? I didn't because, at the end of 2017, I burned out in spectacular fashion in my role as a school counsellor.

That was in an organisation, and I have learned that in private practice, the emotional toll is far more real, as you're on your own, and if you don't actively protect your energy, the price will be high—your business, your clients, and your well-being all at risk.

This chapter is the shortest in the book because it's not designed to be a deep dive into self-care. There are countless excellent books, courses, and resources on burnout, compassion fatigue, vicarious trauma, and work-life balance. Instead, this chapter is about one simple truth: if you don't take care of yourself, your practice won't survive. It's about recognising that self-care isn't a luxury or something to squeeze in when you have time, it's an essential foundation of sustainable private practice.

The wings of your counselling practice represent the two forms of self-care that wrap themselves around to protect and sustain you.

In counselling, we talk about the 'therapeutic relationship' as the foundation of our work. But what we don't always acknowledge is that the person in that relationship—you—needs to be in a state where you can show up fully, ethically, and with the emotional capacity to do the job. When self-care is neglected, everything is affected, your whole life and being.

The Consequences of Ignoring Self-Care

Skipping self-care doesn't just affect you personally, it can put your whole practice at risk. Burnout doesn't hit us all at once, we rarely see it coming; it creeps in slowly, like a low fog. At first, you might just feel a bit more tired or a little drained after sessions. You might become cynical about your work, negative about clients and resent them. Then, before you know it, you're dreading client appointments,

Protective Wings – Self-Care That Prevents and Restores

struggling to focus, making reactive business choices, and wondering what on earth happened!

Reality check: when you're emotionally depleted, your clients feel it too. It impacts your presence, your ability to hold space, and even your clinical judgment. Subtle shifts occur, your patience shortens, your empathy wanes, and eventually, you may start to question whether you even want to continue in private practice. Bottom line, you could even be impaired and not in a suitable place to be working with clients, which means you may be causing harm.

Preventative self-care is what stops this from happening in the first place. It's about having the right strategies in place before burnout becomes inevitable. But no matter how well you prepare, there will still be times when exhaustion hits. That's where restorative self-care comes in, helping you step back, reset, and realign so you can keep going.

First Wing – Preventative Self-Care

Preventative self-care is about stopping the cracks before they appear. It's about making self-care an active, deliberate part of your professional routine because waiting until you're burnt out to take action is too late.

Private practice can be all-consuming. The lines between work and life blur, and suddenly at 10 pm, you're answering 'one more email,' and convincing yourself that your needs can wait. But the reality is, self-care isn't just about you, it directly impacts your ability to be an effective, ethical counsellor who will last the distance, and let's not forget the impact on loved ones.

The Counsellors Chair

The Burnout of Wearing Too Many Hats

Self-care in private practice isn't just about emotional well-being; it's also about recognising the weight of running a business. You're not just the counsellor. You're the admin assistant, bookkeeper, marketer, CEO, social media manager, and crisis response team all in one. And if you're not careful, that weight will crush you. I learned this the hard way.

For years, I tried to juggle everything myself, seeing clients, responding to emails, updating my website, managing finances, and handling bookings. At the end of each day, I was exhausted; not just emotionally, but mentally and physically. The burnout wasn't from the client work itself, it was from trying to do it all and I was resenting my dream as the daily grind was preventing me from developing the big picture.

Eventually, I had to make a choice. I hired a virtual assistant to handle all the social media and marketing in my business. I also now have an admin assistant who does all my invoicing and reconciliation. It wasn't an easy expense to justify, but the freedom it gave me to step back, focus on my clients and supervisees, and focus on being a creative business owner was beyond priceless. I certainly wouldn't have been able to write this book.

Many counsellors I supervise struggle with the same challenge. They love their clinical work, but they're overwhelmed by the business side of private practice. The endless to-do lists, the marketing, the admin—it all piles up until it starts affecting their actual counselling work.

This is why preventative self-care matters. It's about creating boundaries before burnout becomes the default. That includes:

Protective Wings – Self-Care That Prevents and Restores

- Setting clear work hours and sticking to them. Your clients don't expect you to be available 24/7, you're the one making that choice.
- Prioritising supervision and peer support, so you're not carrying the emotional load of your work alone.
- Structuring your business so it supports your well-being, whether that means reducing your caseload, outsourcing admin, or adjusting your schedule.
- Resisting the urge to keep taking on one more client when your schedule is full. We far overestimate what we can achieve in a short space of time and underestimate what we can achieve in a longer period.

Second Wing – Restorative Self-Care

Even with the best preventative strategies in place, there will be times when the wheels fall off the wagon. A difficult client case, financial stress, personal challenges, all of these can drain you, no matter how resilient you are. Restorative self-care is about recognising when you're running on empty, experiencing compassion fatigue or even vicarious trauma and having a plan to recover before it affects your work, your business, and your clients.

Here are some ways to prioritise restorative self-care:

- Know when to step back. If you're exhausted, overwhelmed, or emotionally depleted, reducing your caseload, even temporarily, might be a necessary step.
- Engage in your own therapy when necessary. I believe that *all* counsellors should engage in their own therapy and keep working on themselves. Not all the time, but how do you know what it means to be a client if you've never been one?

Just because you're a counsellor doesn't mean you don't need counselling.
- Adjust your workload. If you're constantly feeling drained, something isn't working. That might mean restructuring your fees, shifting your hours, or even reconsidering your niche.
- Take real breaks. Scrolling social media between sessions isn't rest. Actual disconnection, whether it's a weekend off, a holiday, or just a few hours away from work matters and can make all the difference.
- Know yourself and your personality needs. I'm an introvert, and I need my own space after speaking with people all day. It's vital to my survival, as without it I become snappy, crappy and stressed.

Without restorative self-care, you power through until you crash. You start making reactive business decisions out of exhaustion, disengage from client work, or, worst case scenario, step away from private practice altogether.

Let's Chat About Those Doubts

I see you—I've been there and got the tee shirt (unfortunately)! I know how easy it is to tell yourself, 'I'll rest when I really need it.' But burnout doesn't tap you on the shoulder and give you a warning, it creeps in quietly, disguising itself as just another busy week, just a little more exhaustion than usual. And then suddenly, you're running on fumes, your family are avoiding you and you're questioning if you can keep doing this at all. You don't wait for your car to break down before you service it (I hope). The same goes for you, taking care of yourself isn't a luxury, it's the fuel that keeps your practice running.

Protective Wings – Self-Care That Prevents and Restores

Self-care can feel like just another thing on an already endless to-do list, but this isn't about doing more, it's about doing less of what drains you. Maybe it's cutting back on an overloaded schedule, setting firmer boundaries, or finally outsourcing that admin that's swallowing your time. Sometimes, self-care isn't an action, it's permission to stop, breathe, and restructure before exhaustion forces you to.

Then there's the fear of slowing down, of losing income, of not having enough. But let me ask you this: what happens to your business if you're too depleted to run it? If you're constantly pushing through, seeing clients when you're running on empty, that's not just bad for you, it's unfair to them. They need a counsellor who's present, clear-headed, and capable. You deserve that version of yourself too.

You don't have to overhaul everything overnight. One shift at a time. One healthier boundary. One decision to protect your energy. Future you, the one who still loves this work, who doesn't feel constantly on the edge of burnout, is going to thank you for starting today. You've got this.

How's Counsellor Casey Going?

Casey always knew private practice would be hard work, but they hadn't expected to feel like they were running two full-time jobs, one as a counsellor, the other as an administrator, marketer, bookkeeper, and everything in between. The reality of spinning all these plates was overwhelming. The client work was fulfilling, but the constant behind-the-scenes demands were draining.

'I thought being in private practice meant more freedom and time for myself, I had this idea of easy days! Boy was I wrong. Instead, I felt like I was always working. Between sessions, I was chasing invoices, fixing tech issues, and trying to figure out how to market myself, all while keeping up with my professional development. No matter how much I got done, the to-do list never seemed to shrink.'

The turning point came when Casey realised that being busy didn't mean being productive. The long hours spent struggling through admin weren't adding to the business, they were taking away from it. Instead of growing, they were stuck in survival mode, constantly putting out fires but never moving forward.

'I'd spend hours on things I wasn't even good at, overwhelm would kick in and I would procrastinate and scroll on social media instead. I spent too long designing social media posts, updating my website, and figuring out my accounting software. And the worst part? None of it felt like it was making a real difference. I was exhausted and annoyed, and my partner was getting frustrated at not seeing me.'

After months of frustration, Casey made a shift. They streamlined systems, setting up automated booking and invoicing instead of manually handling everything. Instead of trying to master every aspect of the business, they outsourced the things that were slowing them down, first a bookkeeper, and then later a virtual assistant to handle admin tasks.

'Letting go of control was hard. I told myself I couldn't afford to pay someone else, but the truth was, I couldn't afford not to. The time and energy I got back was worth every cent. I started using that time to focus on what actually mattered, working with clients, refining my skills, and thinking about the future of my practice, instead of just trying to survive the day-to-day.'

For Casey, the biggest lesson wasn't about doing more, it was about doing less of the things that weren't serving the business. By shifting their focus from simply keeping up to something that felt intentional and viable, private practice finally started to feel like the career they had envisioned.

Action Steps

1. Assess Your Workload and Identify One Task to Offload

Take a step back and evaluate the different roles you're juggling in private practice. Identify one administrative or business-related task that's draining your energy and explore options to delegate, automate, or simplify it, whether that means outsourcing, streamlining your systems, or setting firmer boundaries around your time.

2. Create a Personal Check-In

Set aside time each week or fortnight to check in on how you're feeling—your energy levels, stress, and overall well-being. Ask yourself: Am I feeling drained? Am I still enjoying my work? What needs to shift? Ask those close to you if they notice any changes (be willing to hear the answers!). These small check-ins can help you make changes early before burnout creeps in.

3. Set a Recovery Plan for When You Hit the Wall

Burnout isn't always avoidable, but knowing how you'll respond when it happens makes a difference. Write down a simple recovery plan, who you'll turn to for support, what

> restorative activities help you reset, and what changes you'll make to your workload when needed. Having this plan in place will make it easier to step back and regroup when the time comes.

'People learn how to treat us based on how they see us treating ourselves. If I don't put value on my work o my time, neither will the person I'm helping. Boundaries are a function of self-respect and self-love.'

— Brené Brown

AFTERWORD

'Education without application is just entertainment.'
Tim Sanders

Well, here we are. You made it to the end of the book, and that alone says something. Hopefully, you've taken in new ideas, challenged your thinking, and started seeing what's possible for you and your private practice. That's no small thing. I truly hope that as a counsellor in private practice—whatever your stage of that journey—you've felt understood and have resonated with this book.

But here's the truth: reading alone won't change anything, and that's where most people get stuck. It's easy to feel overwhelmed, to second-guess yourself, to wonder if you're doing things 'the right way'.

Here's what I want you to remember: there's no perfect way—only your way.

You don't need to have all the answers. You don't need a flawless plan before you begin. You just need to take the next step. Whether that's revisiting certain chapters, putting strategies into action, or setting small, achievable goals, the key is to keep moving forward.

You can absolutely take what you've learned here and work through it on your own. If that's the path you choose, I truly hope this book gives you clarity and confidence, and I'd love to hear how you go. Send me an email, share your wins, your challenges, your progress—I love hearing how counsellors step into their practice with purpose.

But if you're feeling like you could use some guidance, some accountability, or just a supportive group of people who get it, then know that you don't have to do this alone.

The next few pages will walk you through ways to continue this journey with support—whether that's through supervision, business mentoring, or connecting with a community of counsellors navigating the same path.

However you choose to move forward, know this: you already have what it takes to build a private practice that's fulfilling, ethical, and is going to last the distance. You don't need to have it all figured out today, just start. Take the next step.

Don't forget the famous words of Yoda, 'Try not. Do. Or do not. There is no try.'

And know that I'm cheering you on every step of the way.

NEXT STEPS

'Knowledge is nothing without action. Nothing changes until you do something. What you do will directly determine what you learn.'
James A. Belasco

Whatever stage of the private practice journey you find yourself on, it's time to take the next step in a way that works for you. Whether you need practical tools, a supportive community, guided support, or training, there's an option for you. Wherever you are in your journey, you don't have to do it alone, let's take the next step together.

1. Counsellors Chair Companion Workbook: Your free 92-page workbook, designed to help you apply the concepts from this book with practical exercises and reflections.

2. Counsellors Community Australia: A space to connect, learn, and grow with other counsellors through our free Facebook community or take it deeper in our premium Circle community with exclusive content and ongoing professional development.

3. The Counsellor's Chair Program and Hybrid Membership: For those ready for individualised support, tailored guidance, and structured strategies to build a thriving private practice.

4. Speaking and Workshops: Specialised training for organisations, teams, and events on private practice and supervision, bringing real-world insight and practical strategies to professional development.

Let's journey together through the seasons of your counselling career!

ONE: DOWNLOAD YOUR COUNSELLORS CHAIR COMPANION WORKBOOK

COUNSELLORS CHAIR COMPANION
92 PAGE WORKBOOK

- ✓ YOUR BLUEPRINT TO SET UP YOUR PRACTICE
- ✓ HANDY CHECKLISTS TO KEEP YOU ON TRACK
- ✓ STEP BY STEP ACTION STEPS TO GUIDE YOU

TWO: JOIN COUNSELLORS COMMUNITY AUSTRALIA

COUNSELLORS COMMUNITY AUSTRALIA

1. FREE FACEBOOK COMMUNITY

Join 8k + Counsellors in the largest online community just for Aussie Counsellors

2. PREMIUM CIRCLE COMMUNITY

Join 400+ Counsellors in our enhanced community experience. Live events, training, OPD, resources & more. Low-cost at $27 month or $270 annual. Conditions apply

FB COMMUNITY   WEBSITE

CONTRIBUTE | COLLABORATE | CONNECT

THREE: THE COUNSELLOR'S CHAIR PROGRAM AND HYBRID MEMBERSHIP

BEYOND THE CHAIR

- Actionable Roadmaps
- Recorded Training
- Guest Experts
- Community Forum
- Personal Vault of indivualised support

LEARN MORE

FOUR: SPEAKING, WORKSHOPS AND TRAINING

Penny Adams is a highly experienced speaker, presenter, and industry leader dedicated to supporting Australian counsellors in building sustainable, fulfilling careers. With over 10 years in counsellor education, she has a gift for breaking down complex topics into practical, absorbable content.

A Level 4 ACA Registered Counsellor, PACFA Clinical Member, and ACA College of Supervisors Member, Penny has extensive experience in private practice, education, and supervision. As the founder of Seasons of Life Counselling and co-founder of Counsellors Community Australia, she blends clinical expertise with real-world business knowledge to help counsellors navigate the challenges of private practice and professional growth.

Known for her no-nonsense, down-to-earth style, Penny delivers engaging, insightful presentations with a good dose of humour to keep things light yet impactful. She provides ongoing workshops, training, and supervision to counsellors and supervisors nationwide, ensuring no counsellor navigates this profession alone.

BOOK YOUR EVENT

KEY SPEAKER TOPICS

1. THE COUNSELLORS CHAIR
Building a Thriving Practice

Learn the essentials of creating a sustainable, profitable, and enjoyable counselling practice with clear strategies for business, marketing, and growth.

2. SUPERVISION FOR SUCCESS
Expanding Your Impact & Income

Take your counselling career to the next level by developing an ethical and effective supervision business, supporting counsellors while expanding your own professional opportunities.

3. BEYOND THE THERAPY ROOM
Alternative Income for Counsellors

Discover diverse income streams beyond client sessions, from workshops to digital products, creating financial stability and freedom.

ABOUT THE AUTHOR

Born in the UK, Penny Adams migrated to Australia in 1977 with her parents. The death of both her parents within three months of each other in her early 20s, was immensely painful. A complete lack of mental health support meant the grief and unimaginable loss was overwhelming at times, but nonetheless, tragedy forged the path for Penny's future in counselling. It wasn't until she sought counselling for herself that she realised just how transformative the process could be. That experience planted a seed, a calling to support others as she had been supported.

Counselling is a second career for Penny, after many years working in customer service and retail management. She had spent years honing her ability to connect with people. But it was in counselling, supervision, and community-building that all her experiences and skills came together.

Now an established Level 4 ACA Registered Counsellor, PACFA Clinical Member, and ACA College of Supervisors Member, Penny has dedicated her career to supporting both clients and fellow counsellors across Australia. She holds a Bachelor of Counselling and a Graduate Certificate in Counselling and has worked extensively in education, training, private practice, supervision and supervision on supervision.

Her early counselling career included years as a school counsellor, supporting students through mental health issues, academic pressures, and personal challenges. Penny cares deeply about supporting the next generation of counsellors. She spent seven years training and mentoring students in an RTO, helping them step into their careers with confidence. Along the way, she saw the real gaps; so many counsellors felt unprepared for the business side of things and lacked the industry support they needed to feel like they could succeed.

Penny is the founder of Seasons of Life Counselling, where she focuses on supporting rural and regional South Australians, and has a special interest in FIFO workers and their families. She understands the unique rural challenges of isolation and access to mental health services. As a FIFO partner of 20 years, she understands the unique challenges of this lifestyle. Her work blends compassionate understanding with practical strategies, ensuring clients receive affordable, approachable and accessible counselling to help them navigate the many seasons of life.

Beyond private practice, Penny is the co-founder of Counsellors Community Australia, the largest social media community platform for Aussie counsellors. What began as a Facebook group in 2022 has since expanded into a premium professional development community with over 8,000 members and a dedicated premium Circle community with almost 400 members. Through this platform, with her colleague, Rosie Barbara, Penny provides ongoing education, mentorship, and connection for counsellors across the country, helping them build enjoyable, profitable businesses and navigate their counselling careers.

About the Author

Her passion for the industry extends beyond clinical work—she's committed to helping others succeed in their careers. She believes that counsellors need more than just clinical skills to thrive, they need confidence, business knowledge, and a strong support system.

Penny's own journey hasn't been without challenges. From burnout to personal loss, financial struggles to professional setbacks, she has experienced the real difficulties of being a counsellor in private practice. But through it all, she has stayed true to her values, supported her colleagues, and held to strong ethical practices.

ACKNOWLEDGEMENTS

I want to thank those who have walked alongside me, both professionally and personally, offering wisdom, encouragement, and unwavering friendship, this book is as much yours as it is mine. To my dear friends and colleagues Deb, Peter and Betty, for your ongoing collegial support, wisdom, fun, and guidance. To Colleen, who believed in me in my early school counselling days and helped shape the counsellor I've become.

To my supervisor, Tracey Milson—your mentorship, wisdom, character, kind nudging, and encouragement have pushed me beyond my comfort zone and been a guiding light through the difficult times. You're an inspiration to me.

To Rosie Barbara, my friend, business partner and co-founder of Counsellors Community Australia—we're quite the team, and I am so grateful for your friendship, professionalism, guiding strength, and shared vision for our community.

To Sarah Thomson, business coach extraordinaire—thank you for pulling and pushing me (with both kindness and firmness!) over the last few years. Your insight and marketing knowledge have been invaluable.

To the whole team at the Ultimate 48 Hour Author, that help us create our books and share our vision and stories. I wouldn't have ever got this far without your program—it would have stayed a dream in my head.

And finally, to the wonderful counsellors, seasoned and budding who have trusted me to walk with them on their journey, sharing both triumphs and struggles—this book is for you. It's a privilege to be part of your story as you journey through the seasons of your counselling careers.

MORE TESTIMONIALS

Attending The Fundamentals of Private Practice workshop was an invaluable experience. It provided me with a clear understanding of the essential foundations for building and growing a successful private practice. Before the workshop, I felt lost and unsure about what was required to start my business. Penny's practical advice and expert guidance gave me the confidence and direction I needed to take those first steps. I highly recommend this workshop to anyone navigating the early stages of private practice.

Jessica Day
Counsellor
Endue Counselling Services
www.enduecounsellingservices.com

Attending Penny's private practice workshop was a transformative experience. Her insightful approach and extensive knowledge provided me with practical tools I could implement immediately. The supportive environment fostered open discussions, allowing us to share challenges and successes. Penny's guidance on client management and marketing strategies was invaluable. I left feeling inspired to take my business to the next level. The resources provided were thorough and easy to understand. I highly recommend this workshop to anyone looking to enhance their private practice skills. Thank you, Penny, for an incredible opportunity!

Liana Papoutsis
Counsellor
www.lianapapoutsis.com.au

Penny's training on setting up a private counselling practice was groundbreaking for me.

I didn't know where to start. Penny's step-by-step instructions on things to consider in all areas for business set up were the fundamental steps I needed to begin and made the whole process so much easier to navigate. Penny's top tips in each section were incredibly helpful and the action checklists made everything so simple.

Nicole Tattersall
Counsellor
Wellshore Counselling
www.wellshorecounselling.com.au

NOTES

The Counsellor's Chair

Notes

www.ingramcontent.com/pod-product-compliance
Lightning Source LLC
Chambersburg PA
CBHW030319080526
44584CB00012B/624